The Kemp To Branch Line

Peter A. Harding

Terrier 0-6-0T No.62 *Preston* at Kemp Town Station waiting to run round a train of four-wheeled coaches in the late 1890's.
Lens of Sutton

Published by Peter A. Harding,
"Mossgiel", Bagshot Road, Knaphill,
Woking, Surrey GU21 2SG.

ISBN 0 9523458 4 6

Contents

Introduction   3

History of the Line   4

Description of the Route   15

Motive Power and Rolling Stock   23

Timetables and Tickets   27

Closure   28

The Present Scene   30

Conclusion   31

Acknowledgements   32

Bibliography   32

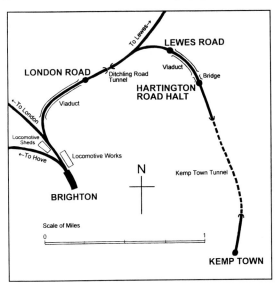

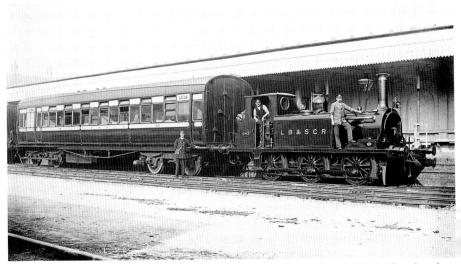

Terrier 0-6-0T No.643, formerly called *Gipsyhill*, at Kemp Town Station with a pull-and-push train comprising of a single trailer coach in about 1916/17. These trains soon became known as 'motor-trains' or 'rail-motors'.
R.C.Riley Collection

Introduction

The short but interesting branch line that connected Brighton with Kemp Town was opened by the London, Brighton & South Coast Railway on August 2nd 1869 and was not only built to serve the Kemp Town area, but also as a defence to stop rival railway companies reaching Brighton via Kemp Town.

The branch left the main Brighton to Lewes line just to the east of the short Ditchling Road Tunnel and was very much a suburban service running through a built up area mostly on an embankment, a viaduct or in a tunnel. On September 1st 1873 a station was opened at Lewes Road which was situated next to the viaduct while on January 1st 1906 a halt was opened at Hartington Road. As the route was of a circular nature, the area within became an easy target for trams and later buses, which were more direct. Although the passenger service was withdrawn on and from January 1st 1933 the goods service surprisingly survived until 1971.

As very little remains to show people that there ever was a branch line that went to Kemp Town, I hope that this booklet provides a gentle reminder to the older generation of times gone by and, gives the younger generation an idea as to what the railway in this part of Brighton was really like.

A two coach special train organised by the Stephenson Locomotive Society arrives at Kemp Town Station from Brighton on June 23rd 1956. The locomotive is Terrier 0-6-0T No.377S called *Brighton Works* but was formerly called *Morden*.   R.C.Riley

3

History of the Line

After several schemes were put forward, the main railway line between London and Brighton received the Royal Assent on July 15th 1837 for a line to be built by the London & Brighton Railway which would join the London & Croydon Railway at a junction near Norwood. This new line would not only connect London and Brighton but would also involve branches from Brighton to Shoreham, Lewes and Newhaven.

On May 12th 1840 the branch between Brighton and Shoreham was the first of these lines to actually open and because of its isolated position from any other completed railway, the engines arrived by sea. The first section of the main line opened from Norwood to Haywards Heath on July 12th 1841 and finally to Brighton on September 21st 1841.

Although the London & Brighton Railway also had powers to build branches to Lewes and Newhaven as well as Shoreham, it was left to the Brighton, Lewes & Hastings Railway in 1844 to obtain authority for the line to Lewes to be built and, under the same Act, to sell the undertaking to the London & Brighton Railway. The line from Brighton to Lewes was opened on June 8th 1846 and then to West Marina at St. Leonards on June 27th 1846. Hastings was later reached on February 13th 1851 over a line built by the South Eastern Railway.

On July 27th 1846, the Royal Assent was given for an Act to amalgamate the London & Croydon Railway and the London & Brighton Railway to become the London, Brighton & South Coast Railway (LBSCR).

In 1845, the Brighton, Lewes & Hastings Railway was granted authority to build a line from Wivelsfield on the main London - Brighton line to Lewes which would give Lewes and St. Leonards direct access to London. This line was opened on October 2nd 1847. The line to Newhaven which was part of the original plan put forward by the London & Brighton Railway in 1837 opened on December 8th 1847.

The town of Brighton was now well and truly on the railway map and perhaps it is not so surprising that other railway company's cast their envious eyes in that direction. With encouragement from the London, Chatham & Dover Railway, a private company submitted proposals to Parliament in 1863 for a line to run from near Beckenham through East Grinstead to Lewes, from where it would gradually curve round to the Kemp Town district of Brighton. After some consideration, the House of Commons committee rejected the proposals but the company still tried again in 1864 also without success.

With all this happening, plus the mention of one or two other similar plans, the LBSCR decided that they should do something about the situation. The Kemp Town area which lays to the east of Brighton had been built by Thomas Read Kemp who commenced building in the early 1820's, and was a magnificent estate built in the regency style. The intention was to attract "fashionable people" out of the already cramped Brighton but, unfortunately for Thomas Read Kemp, who sank the whole of his large fortune in this development, he was unable to complete the project and needed financial help from other builders.

Thomas Read Kemp was born in 1781 and was the son of Thomas Kemp of Lewes Castle and Hurstmonceaux Park, M.P. for Lewes. After his education at St. John's College, Cambridge where he graduated as a B.A. in theology in 1805 and an M.A. in 1810, he too became M.P. for Lewes in May 1811. He retired from Parliament in 1816 to become a preacher, having seceded from the Church of England with his brother-in-law the Rev. George Baring and others to form a religious sect. After attracting some notoriety, this religious sect later fell to pieces and, by 1823 he had returned to the established church.

Kemp had a passion for building and after inheriting and selling the castles at Lewes and Hurstmonceaux and buying Dale Park near Arundel, which he later sold, he built a large house in Montpelier Road, Brighton, which he called 'The Temple' and another at the south-west corner of Belgrave Square, London, which later became the residence of General Lord Hill.

After starting the Kemp Town development, he returned to politics and once again became M.P. for Lewes in 1826 and remained so until he finally retired from Parliament in April 1837. He died suddenly in Paris on December 20th 1844.

The LBSCR obtained authority on May 13th 1864, to construct a 1 mile 32 chains branch to Kemp Town from a junction on the Brighton to Lewes line about a mile from Brighton Station on the east side of the Ditchling Road Tunnel, at an estimated cost of £100,000 (£75,000 in shares and £25,000 in loans). Although the cost for such a short line might on the face of it seem high, it is not really such a surprise as land in this part of Brighton was expensive and the route required not only a 14 arch viaduct over Lewes Road, which was about 180 yards long and 50 feet above the road, but also an extensive bridge over Hartington Road, plus a 1024 yard tunnel from where the line would then emerge from chalk cliffs into the new station at Kemp Town.

The LBSCR engineer at this time was Frederick Dale Banister who had taken over from R.Jacomb-Hood in December 1860. Banister, who was to hold the engineer's position for the next thirty five years, took on this short but heavily engineered branch to Kemp Town with George Parker Bidder, who apart from being much employed in the practice of his profession as an engineer, was also something of a celebrity as a rapid calculator. The *Directory of National Biography* describes him as follows:-

As a child he showed a most extraordinary power of mental calculation, a power that in which he was equalled by few and perhaps surpassed by none who have ever lived.

As an engineer, Bidder constructed numerous railways and other works at home and abroad. The Victoria Docks (London) are considered one of his chief constructive works, while he was the originator of the railway swing bridge, the first of which was designed and erected by him at Reedham on the Norwich and Lowestoft Railway.

The contractors appointed to build the branch to Kemp Town were William & Jonathan Pickering who, it is understood hired from the LBSCR a 0-6-0 tender engine, No.112 which was built by Stothert & Slaughter in January 1847 to use for the construction.

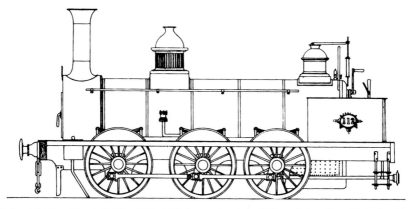

Stothert & Slaughter 0-6-0 No.112 which the contractors William & Jonathan Pickering hired from the LBSCR for use on the construction of the branch.

It is interesting to note that at about the same time as they took on the Kemp Town project, the combination of Banister, Bidder and William & Jonathan Pickering were also given the task of building the ill-fated Ouse Valley line which was to run from the Ouse Viaduct, north of Haywards Heath on the main London to Brighton line, to Uckfield on the Tunbridge Wells to Brighton line, and then on to Hailsham. At about this time, the LBSCR ran into financial problems and the Ouse Valley line was abandoned even though it was partly constructed. Powers to terminate the project were finally obtained in 1868.

Work on the Kemp Town branch officially got under way on February 17th 1866, when the Mayor of Brighton, Alderman Henry Martin turned the first sod to commemorate the occasion. With such enormous engineering problems to face, it is not so surprising that such a short branch took to so long to build. In fact it was not until July 1869 that the line was ready for inspection by the Board of Trade. Col. Yolland carried out the inspection on July 9th 1869 and said he was "more than satisfied".

The line opened to the public on Monday August 2nd 1869 and the Tuesday August 3rd 1869 edition of the *Brighton Examiner* gave the following report:-

OPENING OF THE KEMP TOWN BRANCH OF THE BRIGHTON RAILWAY -YESTERDAY.
The opening for public passenger traffic, of the Kemp Town branch of the London, Brighton, and South Coast railway, which has been for some time in course of construction, took place yesterday, without any special formality. The new station, which is immediately behind Steam Mills in the Eastern-road, and almost behind the College, is an appropriately handsome building, containing all the necessary offices, waiting rooms, and station master's residence, and is approached from the Eastern-road by two good roads - Park-road East, which leads past the Park wall to the Race-course, and by the road which separates it from the College grounds leading to it past Evershed's candle factory. Within the station is a long platform and excellent shed, permitting every convenience for taking up or landing passengers, leading into a short cutting, at the end of which is the opening of the tunnel, by which the line is carried through Race-hill, emerging to the north of the old road leading from the Lewes line near the north entrance of the Round-hill tunnel. The whole distance from the Terminus, by the new branch line to the Kemp-town station, is not far short of two miles, of which something more than a quarter of a mile is occupied by the tunnel we have mentioned. The line is at present single, but as it has been arranged never to have but one train on the line, going or returning, any collision will be impossible. A very brief notice has been given of the opening of the line, which has, we surmise, been determined on for the occasion of the Brighton Races, to the visitors to which, residing at the central or western parts of the town, or arriving at the Terminus, it will be an accommodation, the walk or ride from the Kemp Town Station to the Race Course being but short, compared with the distance from the Terminus, and some portion of the hill will be avoided. Trains have been announced to run to and fro on the branch nine times a day, in connection with the trains arriving at and departing from the Terminus, and the fares being very moderate, will doubtless be an inducement to the public to use the line, and to establish a large and steady traffic.

The formal ceremony to mark the opening took place on Friday August 6th 1869, when the former Mayor Mr. Alderman Martin laid the last brick in the eastern pier of the central arch of the Lewes Road Viaduct, thus completing the task he started as Mayor of Brighton on February 17th 1866, when he turned the first sod.

This special occasion and the banquet which followed at the Old Ship Hotel were reported in the Saturday August 7th 1869 edition of the *Brighton Herald* as follows :-

COMPLETION OF THE KEMP-TOWN BRANCH RAILWAY
The Kemp-town Branch of the London, Brighton, and South-Coast railway was opened to the public last Monday, as we announced last week would be the case; but it was not till yesterday that the finishing stroke was given to the works.
Yesterday, the last brick was laid by Mr. Alderman Martin, under the superintendence, as it were, of Mr. William Pickering, the senior partner of the firm who constructed the Line; this task being performed by Mr. Martin because the work had been commenced by him during his Mayoralty, three years ago. The brick having been placed in its position, in the eastern pier of the central arch of the viaduct which spans the Lewes-road, Mr. Pickering handed a silver trowel

to Mr. Martin to finish off the work, expressing a hope that it would not be the last labour of the kind which he would be called upon to perform.

(The trowel, - which was massive silver of elegant design, and most elaborately and exquisitely engraved and chased, - bore the following inscription: - "Presented to Mr. Alderman Martin by the Contractors, Wm. and Jno. Pickering, in commemoration of his turning the first sod of the Kemp Town Branch Railway on 17th day of February, 1866, as Mayor of Brighton, and finished by him on the 6th of August, 1869.")

Mr. Alderman Martin, having terminated his labours, said he had now to pronounce the last brick laid of the Kemp-town Branch railway. When Mayor of Brighton, three years ago, he had the honour of turning the first sod; and had had the happy privilege of living to see the work completed. (Hear, hear.) He wished to be permitted to say that it was to the credit of Mr.William and Mr.Jonathan Pickering, the contractors, that the Company and the public were indebted for the substantial manner in which the work had been carried out; and the attractions which already existed in Brighton. He also trusted that it would be remunerative to the Shareholders, hoping that they would have no cause to regret that this extension of their system had been made; and he congratulated them upon the fact that it had been so satisfactorily finished. (Hear, hear.) To Mr. William Pickering, who had presented him with this very handsome trowel, Mr. Martin expressed his personal thanks, stating that he should ever cherish the gift on behalf of those who presented it, and as a memento of the confidence which the Company had in them. He hoped it would be retained by his family as an heirloom, descending with other things which he had received, and regarded by those who became possessed of them with the same feelings with which he accepted them. (Cheers)

Mr. William Marchant, who was present, witnessing the proceedings, said he hoped that the Branch Line to Kemp Town would not only be remunerative to the Shareholders but a benefit to the east end of Brighton, which, in some respects, - if it had not been entirely left out in the cold, - had not been so prosperous as the west end. He sincerely hoped that it would be made a public benefit, and induce persons to take up their abode at the east end; and he also hoped that the Company would take into consideration the desirability of making a Station near the spot on which they were then standing, as it was a large, important, and increasing district, to which an easier access to both east and west of Brighton was highly important and absolutely necessary. (Hear, hear.)

Three cheers for the Contractors terminated the proceedings.

After the ceremony, Messrs. W. and J. Pickering entertained a few of their friends at the Old Ship Hotel to a most *recherché* banquet, at which the Mayor of Brighton (Alderman T. Lester) filled the chair, and Mr. Alderman H. Martin the Vice-chair. Amongst the guests were Messrs. Knight (Traffic Manager of the London, Brighton, and South Coast Railway), J.C.Craven (Locomotive Superintendent), Banister (Engineer), Steer (Accountant), Walker (Station Superintendent), Alderman Cox, W.Marchant, Lutley, C.Fleet, H.Martin, jun., & c. After the usual loyal toasts, the health of Mr. Bidder, the Engineer of the new branch, was proposed from the chair, and acknowledged by Mr. Banister. Mr. Ald. Martin then gave the health of the Contractors of the line, to which Messrs. W. and J. Pickering responded, and this was followed by the toast of the London, Brighton, and South-Coast Railway, proposed by Alderman Cox, and acknowledged by Mr. Knight. Mr. Cox, whilst withholding any opinion on the necessity of a second line, expressed his belief that the existing line had been served as efficiently as it was possible for any line to be served, and paid a high compliment to the late Traffic Manager, Mr. George Hawkins, whose conduct would, he hoped, be emulated by his successor. In acknowledging the toast, which his name was coupled, Mr. Knight expressed the pleasure he had, and always should have, to meet the people of Brighton, to compare notes and come to a mutual understanding. It would, he said, be most gratifying to the Directors to know that their management of the line was appreciated. It was their desire to meet the wants of Brighton in every possible way, and to develop to its fullest extent the traffic between the metropolis and the most important watering place of England. At present they were in a state of transition; but when they had tided over their most pressing difficulties, their consideration would be given to that most important question - a reduction of fares. This was not such a simple matter as it might appear to many, for a change at one place had to be adjusted to others. But they did intend, at the earliest possible time, to give their attention to a revision of fares to such an extent as would be compatible with the interests of the line. Mr. Knight concluded by announcing that the report of the Government Inspector on the Kemp Town branch had been of a most favourable character. Mr. Craven having proposed "the Town and Trade of Brighton" which was acknowledged by Mr. Marchant, and the health of the Mayor having been proposed by Mr. Alderman Martin, and acknowledged by His Worship, the health of the ladies, coupled with the name of Mrs W. Pickering, proposed by Mr. H. Martin. Jun., brought to a close a most agreeable evening.

It is not clear which locomotive was actually used for the first train on the branch as the special engine intended to work from the opening did not arrive from Sharp Stewart & Company until October 1869. This was a small 2-4-0 tank numbered 96, and was ordered by the LBSCR locomotive superintendent Mr. J.C.Craven.

All three classes of passengers were carried and it is interesting to note that the fare to Kemp Town for the 2¼ mile journey from Brighton was 6d (old pence) for single first class and 9d return, while third class was 2d single and 4d return. As there were no intermediate stations, the journey took about ten minutes.

During the opening ceremony at the Lewes Road Viaduct, Mr. William Marchant mentioned (as reported in the *Brighton Herald*) that he hoped consideration would be given by the LBSCR to building a station in that part of Brighton. Although this request was not instantly answered a station which adjoined the viaduct was opened and appropriately called Lewes Road Station, on September 1st 1873. On October 1st 1877 a further station known as London Road was opened on the Brighton to Lewes line just west of the Ditchling Road Tunnel and, although this new station was on the main line, it also served the Kemp Town branch.

Members of the Lewes Road Congregational Church wait on the up platform at Lewes Road Station on July 5th 1909 for a special train to take them on a church outing. Note how the station adjoins the viaduct (left of photograph). Lens of Sutton

During the early 1900's, many suburban railway routes were beginning to feel the competition of street tramcars and as a way of answering this problem the LBSCR surprisingly introduced a petrol railcar service on the Kemp Town line unlike the steam railcars which at that time were being tried on many country branch lines. This also meant that a new halt to serve local residents and the nearby cemetery was opened at Hartington Road between Lewes Road Station and the Kemp Town Tunnel on Monday January 1st 1906. In fact, the revised timetable showed that it was only two minutes from Lewes Road Station to Hartington Road Halt and from there it was only three minutes to Kemp Town Station via the tunnel. Unfortunately, the LBSCR opened this new halt without informing the Board of Trade who only found out when the following article appeared in the December 18th 1905 edition of *The Times*:-

RAIL MOTOR SERVICE BETWEEN BRIGHTON AND KEMP TOWN

The London, Brighton & South Coast Railway Company are about to substitute rail motor cars on their branch line between Brighton and Kemp Town for the existing trains of the ordinary first, second, and third class type of carriage. The new service, which will begin on January 1st next, is a considerable improvement. It will be performed by petrol-driven cars, of one class only, capable of seating 48 passengers. A platform has been erected between Kemp Town and Lewes-road, to be known as "Hartington-road Halt", where all cars will call to take up and set down passengers. Passengers travelling from the stations must obtain tickets at the booking office in the usual way before beginning the journey, but persons joining at the "halt" must obtain them from the conductor in charge of the car. Twenty nine journeys will be made each way on weekdays and 26 on Sundays, in place of 17 journeys on weekdays and six on Sundays, as at present. An endeavour has been made to give a half-hour service throughout the day, but it was found impracticable without interference with important main line trains.

This cutting from *The Times* plus a new Timetable which the LBSCR had issued giving details of the new Hartington Road Halt and the latest train times to start from Monday January 1st 1906 were sent to the LBSCR by the Board of Trade on January 2nd 1906 asking the LBSCR to explain why they had not been informed and why they had not requested the new "halt " to be inspected. The LBSCR Company Secretary Mr. J. J. Brewer answered with this somewhat embarrassing reply:-

Sir,
I have to acknowledge your letter of yesterdays date calling attention to the fact that the Company has brought into use for passenger traffic a Motor Halt at Hartington Road between Brighton and Kemp Town, and that the work has not been inspected by the Board of Trade. The Halt in question is constructed on exactly similar lines to others which have been inspected and passed by the Board of Trade; no alteration of permanent way has been made, and there are no signals, and in these circumstances the Company did not think it necessary to trouble the Board of Trade, but I am to express regret that this was a mistaken view and that notice was not given, and to say that the responsible officers are at the disposal of the Inspecting Officer at any time which may be convenient. In the meantime it is hoped that the Board will not object to the Halt being kept open and used.

An Edwardian view of Hartington Road looking up towards the railway bridge. The Halt was approached by a footpath from the road to the right of the photograph just in front of the bridge.

The Board of Trade quickly arranged to have Hartington Road Halt inspected and this was carried out on January 5th 1906 by Col. von Donop who was quite satisfied with the arrangement. Col. von Donop mentioned in his report that:-

It was a platform 150 feet long, 7 feet wide and 3 feet high, has been constructed on one side of the line. It is provided with lamp, name board and a suitable road of approach.

The petrol railcars were not a success and when unfortunately three pistons penetrated the crankcase of railcar No.4 in the Kemp Town Tunnel, terrifying the passengers, they were soon replaced by the introduction of pull-and-push trains.

Hartington Road Halt did not last much longer than the petrol railcars although when the LBSCR announced their intention of closing it, the following item appeared in the June 3rd 1911 edition of the *Brighton Herald:-*

THE HARTINGTON ROAD HALT

Reversing a previous decision on receipt of further information, the General Purpose Committee now decided that the memorial signed by 96 persons and other representations with reference to the proposed closing of Hartington Road Halt be forwarded to the General Manager of the Railway Company, and that the Directors be asked to reconsider the question of closing and removing the Halt.

Unfortunately, the hopes of the "96 persons and other representations" were not considered strong enough to keep the Halt open and it was quietly closed sometime in June 1911, the exact day being uncertain.

Petrol railcar No.4 at Kemp Town Station.   Author's Collection

Terrier 0-6-0T No.79 *Minories* with a trailer coach at Hartington Road Halt in 1906.

From a drawing by the author

The petrol railcars had introduced a one class only ticket and when the pull-and -push trains took over the duty, it was decided to make the branch a third class only service with the exception of one morning and two evening services which connected with London trains, on weekdays only. This arrangement was to last until the branch finally closed to passengers.

As a wartime economy, all services were temporary withdrawn on the branch from January 1st 1917 and while the passenger services were re-instated by September 1st 1919, the goods services were not fully restored until January 2nd 1922.

The temporary withdrawal of the passenger service proved to be disastrous to the branch, as many people had turned to the recently introduced and more direct motor bus services and the already existing trams, and despite increasing the amount of weekday trains to 36 it was all too late. Lewes Road Station had already been reduced to an unstaffed halt with tickets being issued by the conductor/guard on the train but, when the LBSCR became part of the newly formed Southern Railway at the 1923 grouping, the future really looked dim.

The Southern Railway decided to withdraw the passenger service on and from January 1st 1933. The last trains ran on December 31st 1932, the same day as the last steam passenger trains ran on the London to Brighton line before electrification. The Brighton to Lewes line was electrified on July 7th 1935.

This now left the Kemp Town branch as a goods only line and in fact on July 29th 1933, the branch ceased to be worked as a section and became officially regarded as a siding to be worked by one engine in steam with the signal boxes at Kemp Town and Lewes Road closing.

From then onwards the line settled down to one or two goods trains per day plus the occasional sunday school special which seems to have been a tradition on the branch. Although the goods yard was retained at Lewes Road Station, a unique transformation happened at the former station building when the Victor Sauce Company took it over and turned it into a pickle factory. Later, the station became a builder's yard.

The former Lewes Road Station in use as a pickle factory after the line had closed to passengers.
Author's Collection

11

The terminus at Kemp Town was kept very busy in 1935 with full truck loads of general goods which comprised mainly of bricks, lime, cement and sand while nearly 22,000 tons of coal was also received. This was for local merchants who held wharf spaces, although about 100 tons of coke for Portslade was dealt with weekly. Figures for 1935 show that over 6,500 loaded wagons were received while 700 loaded wagons were sent out. Also situated at the Kemp Town terminus at that time was the Associated Biscuit Manufacturers' Depot which was a distribution centre for almost the whole of Sussex, and operated from the old goods shed, plus a new garage which was erected.

During the second world war, the Kemp Town Tunnel was used nightly as an air raid shelter for electric multiple unit trains from October 1941 until May 1944 apart from a few weeks in May and June 1943 when the London Road Viaduct was damaged as a result of enemy bombs. These electric multiple unit trains were hauled by steam from the main line to the tunnel. In the small hours of October 22nd 1943 a high explosive bomb fell 150 yards from the Brighton end of the Kemp Town Tunnel, thereby marooning six electric multiple units stabled in the tunnel. The line was cleared just after mid-day but it must have adversely affected whatever commuter traffic there may have been at that time. Set No. 3034 sustained slight damage.

After the war, the line continued to receive its daily goods trains plus the occasional troop special and in 1948 passed into the hands of the British Railways Southern Region after nationalisation. Surprisingly, the line still remained open to goods traffic and, during the 1950's and 1960's became popular with various railway societies, notably the Railway Correspondence & Travel Society who arranged visits on October 5th and 19th 1952, to celebrate the centenary of Brighton Works.

Guard Will Crawforth on the Railway Correspondence & Travel Society special train at Kemp Town Station. October 5th 1952. John H. Meredith

The Stephenson Locomotive Society special train prepares to leave Kemp Town Station for Brighton. June 23rd 1956. R.M.Casserley

Terrier 0-6-0T No.32636 with the Railway Correspondence & Travel Society special train for Kemp Town between the branch junction and Lewes Road. October 5th 1952. Denis Cullum

Q class 0-6-0 No.30530 passing the site of Hartington Road Halt with a special train for Kemp Town. October 18th 1964. S.C.Nash

33 class No.D6529 pulls a Southern Counties Touring Society special train from the tunnel at Kemp Town Station. October 22nd 1967. John A.M.Vaughan

On January 8th 1963 an E4 class 0-6-2 T No.32468 engine was working the 8.00 a.m. goods train from Brighton when it ran through the buffers at Kemp Town Station and embedded itself in the station buildings. The *Evening Argus* of that day reported this unfortunate incident as follows:-

A 50 ton shunting engine ploughed into Kemp Town Goods Station demolishing buffers, part of the platform and the station office today. The engine, pulling loaded trucks weighing another 120 tons, skidded on the ice covered lines as it approached the station.

The driver, Mr. John Wood and his fireman James Myers, were taken to the Royal Sussex County Hospital for a check-up. Brighton firemen were called to put out the engine's fire and reduce steam pressure in case of an explosion. Later they cleared the wreckage.

Two of the station staff had a lucky escape. Mr. Albert Streeter, of St. Peter's Street, Brighton, and Mr. William Speed, of Donald Hall Road, Brighton, left the office about two minutes before the crash. "I must have had a premonition or something" said Mr. Streeter. "We are normally in the office at that time, but this morning we decided to go and check over some goods trucks".

Lorry driver Maurice Cole, of Lansdown Place, Hove, who was loading bricks at the station, said: "I saw the wheels skidding and knew there had to be a crash. It cut into the station like a bacon slicer. The noise was like a bomb going off".

The line was finally closed on June 26th 1971 when a diesel electric unit ran every hour taking passengers between Brighton and Kemp Town to mark the occasion.

A former Southern Railway utility van in use as the "Goods Enquiry Office" at Kemp Town Station. April 22nd 1967.   G.R.Croughton

E4 class 0-6-2T No.32486 with an up goods train from Kemp Town Station. July 30th 1951.
S.C.Nash

Description of the Route

Unlike many picturesque rural branch lines, the Kemp Town branch was very much a suburban line that was mainly on a viaduct or in a tunnel but, nevertheless it still had very much its own character. Trains would leave Brighton Station from the short bay platform on the extreme east side of the station, and travel on the Lewes line over the London Road Viaduct before reaching London Road Station. This station is of course still on the Brighton to Lewes line but was also the first stop for passengers on their way to Kemp Town. Opened on October 1st 1877, the station has staggered platforms which are joined by a subway, the up platform is 459 ft long while the down platform is 449 ft long. At one time there were three sidings on the down side and one siding on the up side but, these have in more recent times, been removed. A footbridge, which crosses over the station and platforms is in fact a public right of way.

Terrier 0-6-0T No.655 *Stepney* prepares to leave Brighton Station with the branch train for Kemp Town in 1901.   Author's Collection

E5 class 0-6-2T No.2592 arrives at the down platform at London Road Station with a main line train for Tunbridge Wells West in October 1933. This station was also the first stop for Kemp Town passenger trains.   Lens of Sutton

15

From London Road Station the line to Lewes continues through the 63 yard long Ditchling Road Tunnel before immediately reaching the junction for **Kemp Town** which was 76 chains from Brighton. The line to Kemp Town which was 1 mile 32 chains in length from this point, branched off to the right from the Lewes line where a signal box was situated and, continued as a double track, dropping down a 1 in 100 gradient to Lewes Road Station, which had an unusual arrangement of a 293 ft long island platform between the up and down lines and a main 268 ft long platform serving the up line only. A footbridge linked the island platform to the up platform and main station building. A signal box was positioned on the down side just before the line became single and crossed over the 14 arch viaduct. After the passenger service was withdrawn, the down line from the junction through to the station was lifted and the platform footbridge removed. The signal box was also taken out of use and removed.

The handover of the train staff for Kemp Town at the junction signal box. The locomotive is 2MT class 2-6-2T No.41287 with the "Sussex Downsman" special train. 22nd March 1964.

Edwin Wilmshurst

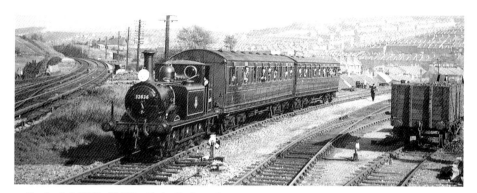

Terrier 0-6-0T No.32636 with the Railway Correspondence & Travel Society special train from Kemp Town approaching the junction. October 5th 1952. Lens of Sutton

View from a goods train leaving the branch at the junction. Lewes Road Station can just be seen in the background. June 30th 1951. D.W.Winkworth

Looking towards the junction from Lewes Road Station. August 23rd 1952. R.C.Riley

Lewes Road Station looking towards Kemp Town after the passenger service had been withdrawn. By this time the down track and footbridge had been removed. 15th March 1952. D.W.Winkworth

Looking from the other side of the station towards the junction. 23rd August 1952. R.C.Riley

This view of the viaduct shows the track curving towards Kemp Town. 23rd August 1952. R.C.Riley

The viaduct from the road. 23rd August 1952. R.C.Riley

Looking back across the viaduct to Lewes Road Station. 23rd August 1952. R.C.Riley

After crossing over the viaduct on the level, the line continued on an elevated embankment and passed over the bridge which crossed Hartington Road. On the Kemp Town side of Hartington Road was the short lived Hartington Road Halt which was a 150 ft long wooden platform built on the up side of the line only. It was typical of several other wooden halts that the LBSCR had built in the area at that time to answer the ever increasing competition from the local electric tramways. Unfortunately the halt was not a success and was only open from January 1st 1906 until June 1911.

← To Lewes Road   To Kemp Town →

HARTINGTON ROAD HALT

Terrier 0-6-0T No.32636 with the Railway Correspondence & Travel Society special train for Kemp Town, passing the site of Hartington Road Halt (left of train). October 5th 1952.   S.C.Nash

Diesel shunter 09 class 0-6-0 No.D3720 with a single coal wagon and a brake van for Kemp Town having just crossed over the bridge at Hartington Road. July 6th 1969.   John A.M.Vaughan

From here the line remained on the level in a cutting before entering the 1,024 yard long Kemp Town Tunnel in which the line dropped down a 1 in 213. On emerging on the level from the tunnel, Kemp Town Station and goods yard was reached which gave the impression of being partly in a big quarry. A signal box was originally situated next to the tunnel but like the one at Lewes Road, it was taken out of use after the passenger service was withdrawn. The station layout consisted of a rather impressive station building which surprisingly had only one main platform which was 481 ft long. The goods and coal yard was quite extensive.

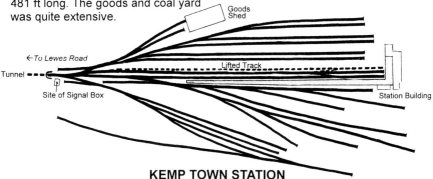

KEMP TOWN STATION

The signal box by the tunnel during passenger days. *Author's Collection*

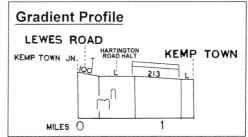

The exterior of Kemp Town Station. October 1949. *T.Middlemass Collection*

Kemp Town Station before the passenger service was withdrawn. Note the long platform cover.
June 1923.   Author's Collection

After the passenger service was withdrawn, the long platform cover was later removed.
August 23rd 1952.   R.C.Riley

Motive Power and Rolling Stock

As mentioned in the history of the line, it is not clear which type of locomotive was used to work the very first train on the branch but, it is known that Mr.J.C.Craven, the LBSCR Locomotive Superintendent at the time, obtained from Sharp Stewart & Co. in October 1869 a 2-4-0T (No.96) specially to work the line. Whether No.96 went straight to the branch is uncertain as some reports say that it worked in the London area for a while. Later this locomotive was overhauled by William Stroudley who became the LBSCR Locomotive Superintendent in 1870, and was put to use on the branch in early 1872, and named *Kemptown*. In June 1874, this small engine was sent to work the Hayling Island branch and was renamed *Hayling Island*.

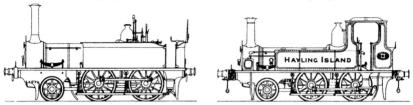

Sharp Stewart 2-4-0T No.96 when it first worked on the branch (left) and after it was modified by William Stroudley (right). It was first called *Kemptown* and later *Hayling Island*.

The replacement for the Kemp Town branch was a Stroudley designed "Terrier" A class 0-6-0T No.64 which also took over the name *Kemptown* and worked both passenger and goods trains. Fellow "Terriers" *Preston* and *Piccadilly* arrived in October 1875 and June 1874 respectively and from then on all three "Terriers" worked not only the Kemp Town branch but also the Seaford branch. By the 1890's several other "Terriers" also worked the line with the occasional appearance of a Stroudley D1 class 0-4-2T. The passenger trains normally consisted of a five-coach close-coupled set of Stroudley four-wheel coaches.

Terrier class 0-6-0T No.64 *Kemptown* in the mid-1890's.   R.Stumpf Collection

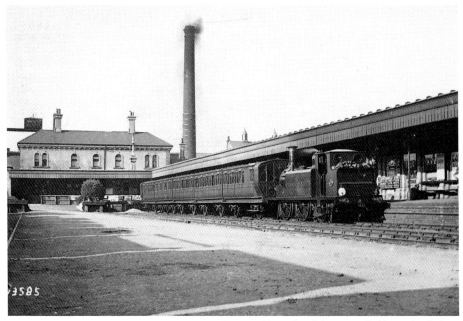

D1 class 0-4-2T No.28 *Isfield* at Kemp Town Station with a train of close-coupled four-wheeled coaches c. 1902.   R.C.Riley Collection

As previously mentioned, in 1905 a petrol railcar service was introduced when Hartington Road Halt was opened and as we have also read, was not a success and was soon withdrawn. The four-wheel 48-seat petrol railcars were obtained from Dick,Kerr and Co, and were No.3 and No.4 following on in sequence from the two steam railcars No.1 and No.2 which the LBSCR had obtained from Beyer, Peacock and Co.

Petrol railcar No.3 which was slightly different from No.4 (see page 10) inasmuch as the windows were more of a classical style.   Author's Collection

From then onwards the service returned to the more than capable "Terriers", some of which were fitted with a form of mechanical control for working pull-and-push trains designed by Douglas Earle Marsh, who had become the LBSCR Locomotive Superintendent in 1905. These trains were often referred to as 'motor-trains' or 'rail-motors' and worked in conjunction with large high-roofed saloon trailers which, as a result of the contrast in size with the small locomotives became known as "balloons". One such trailer with a "Terrier" was usually sufficient to cover the needs of the Kemp Town branch. After Lawson B. Billinton succeeded Douglas Earle Marsh in 1911 he adapted the pull-and-push apparatus to air control, which later became the standard practice throughout the Southern Railway.

The "Terriers" and the occasional D1 class 0-4-2T's continued to work passenger trains until the service was withdrawn by the Southern Railway on January 1st 1933, while the goods trains were normally worked by E4 class 0-6-2T's. This type of locomotive continued to work the goods service after passenger closure although the occasional E3 and E5 class 0-6-2T's and even a Q class 0-6-0 were also seen on duty. When the last E4 class 0-6-2T left Brighton for scrap in June 1963 the goods service was mainly handled by 08 or 09 class 0-6-0 350hp diesel shunters.

Terrier 0-6-0T No.647 formerly called *Cheapside* with its "balloon" trailer at Kemp Town Station July 31st 1926. In April 1912 No.647 had been converted to an A1X class. The late H.C.Casserley

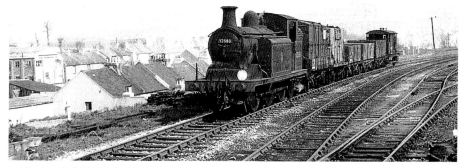

E5 class 0-6-2T No.32583 leaves Lewes Road Station with a short goods train from Kemp Town in 1954. Peter Hay

E3 class 0-6-2T No.32165 arrives at Kemp Town Station with a goods train. September 1953.
Peter Hay

09 class 0-6-0 No.D3720 arrives at the junction with a train of coal wagons from Kemp Town. July 6th 1969.
John A.M.Vaughan

Timetables and Tickets

1890

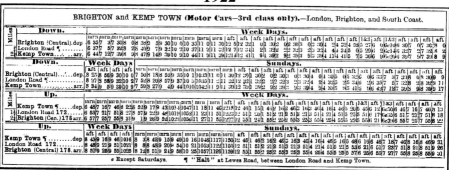

1922

Tickets from the G.R.Croughton Collection.

Closure

When the last passenger train ran over the branch on December 31st 1932 there seems to have been no great celebration to mark the event. The main reason was no doubt that the last official day for steam passenger trains on the London to Brighton line also took place on the same day prior to the new electric service being introduced on the following day. Also, as the goods service was to continue to Kemp Town and the track was not being pulled up, many people probably thought that the passenger service could easily be reintroduced should it be required.

As it was, the goods service lasted until June of 1971 by which time the terminus at Kemp Town had become "Brighton East Goods Depot". After it was announced that the line would close and that the goods service would transfer to Hove, it was decided to run a special commemorative all day passenger service from Brighton on June 26th 1971. The following report from the *Evening Argus* of the same day actually appeared before the last train had left Brighton for Kemp Town:-

KEMP TOWN RETURN

The last trains from Brighton to Kemp Town left platform nine today. The first of them was five minutes late. But it was all smiles from the passengers, almost spilling out of the windows, as Britain's Railway Queen, Miss Lynette Storr, blew a 100-year-old bone whistle to set them on their way.

The passenger service was closed in 1932, and since then only goods trains have used the line. Now the goods facilities are moving to Hove and the line is not needed. Brighton Corporation wants to buy Kemp Town station and develop part of it as an industrial centre.

After a last look round it was back on the train for the return journey through the 1024 yard tunnel under Elm Grove School.

Enthusiasts from all parts of the country formed queues at the barrier and took photographs of Evening Star - the last steam locomotive built by British Rail, which was on display - while they waited for the diesel electric train to haul them to Kemp Town.

Among the many travellers on the three-coach train was Dr. Ian Ronald Phelps, vicar of St. Luke's, Queens Park, who discovered he lived directly above the tunnel when British Rail workmen traced dripping in the tunnel to his burst water pipe. He found the journey interesting - but crowded.

For one-year-old Mark Yarnton, of Greenfield Close, Patcham, it was his first train journey. His rail-enthusiast father thought it would be nice for him to take his first journey on a last run.

Musician Anthony Purkiss, 27, of Newtown Road, Hove, was one of the few travellers who dared to say the ride was bumpy.

Stamp collectors bought specially-designed envelopes, featuring the Terrier locomotive *Kemp Town* for sending on the last train. The envelopes were to be cancelled by hand by the Post Office.

The rail service was operated by volunteer railwaymen to raise money for the Woking Homes for Children and Old People, a railway charity.

Trains were leaving Brighton every hour on the hour and Kemp Town every hour on the half hour. The fare (25p return, 15p for children) will be raised to 50p return for the last train at 9 p.m.

Last trains to Kemptown

Saturday 26 June 1971

Trains will run every hour between
Brighton and Kemptown from 10.00 to 21.00
Journey takes 10 minutes

RETURN FARE
25p Adult   15p Children (3 and under 14)

SPECIAL LAST TRAIN
Leaving Brighton 2100
50p Return fare (no reduction for children)
You can post a letter in a specially designed commemorative
envelope at a small extra charge.

DISPLAY AT BRIGHTON STATION OF 'EVENING STAR'
the last steam locomotive built by British Rail
Admission 10p

Details and reservations from:
Mr. D. E. Plummer, Assistant Station Manager, Brighton station BN1 3XP
or telephone Brighton 26211 Ext 388

ALL PROCEEDS WILL BE DONATED TO THE
SOUTHERN RAILWAYMEN'S WOKING HOMES

British Rail Southern

After the line closed, Brighton Council bought the whole branch from British Rail, which included the stations at Kemp Town and Lewes Road, the viaduct, the bridge over Hartington Road and the tunnel, all amounting to some 17½ acres for an undisclosed figure, and then had to decide what to do with it. Suggestions ranged from helping the congested Brighton traffic problem by turning the line into a relief road, to turning the tunnel into a giant mushroom farm. After much discussion, it was decided to turn the 7³/₄ acres site of Kemp Town Station into an industrial estate. The bridge over Hartington Road was demolished on December 2nd 1973 by an eight-man demolition team from Tarring Contractors of Worthing and the cutting from near the bridge to the tunnel was filled in to make a children's playground. As the goods yard at Lewes Road was also earmarked as an industrial site, the viaduct was demolished in April 1976 leaving just the western arches which were later removed in 1983.

The final special train was diesel electric unit No.1205, seen here passing the site of Hartington Road Halt on the way to Kemp Town. June 26th 1971.   Edwin Wilmshurst

The same special train at Kemp Town Station.   S.C.Nash

The Present Scene

Since the line was closed, very little remains to remind people that a railway line once went to Kemp Town. All traces of the junction off the main Brighton to Lewes line to the east of the short Ditchling Road Tunnel have been completely removed and this area now forms the Centenary Industrial Estate. The Vogue gyratory road layout and the Sainsbury superstore are now situated on what was the site of Lewes Road Station and the viaduct and, although all signs of the railway have now long gone, the Sainsbury superstore does at least incorporate an inbuilt archway design along the side of the building.

A reminder of the line can also be seen in Hartington Road where a building for elderly residents called "Old Viaduct Court" has been built on the Kemp Town side of the embankment where the bridge crossed over the road. From here it is possible to walk up the side of "Old Viaduct Court" to the play area which is built on the filled-in cutting. The sealed northern portal of the tunnel is now in part of the school grounds in Elm Grove.

The whole Kemp Town Station site is now the Freshfield Industrial Estate and the only reminder of the former use of the area is the sealed southern end of the tunnel.

The sealed southern end of the Kemp Town Tunnel, now located in the Freshfield Industrial Estate. October 16th 1998.   Author

Conclusion

Looking back, it is hard to believe that the LBSCR were so worried that other railway companies were likely to reach Kemp Town that they invested so much time and money in such a short line. As a local service with such a circular route it is not so surprising that the passenger service should lose out first to the local street trams, followed by the far more direct buses. Nevertheless, even after the passenger service closed in 1932 the goods service managed to carry on until 1971 proving that the railway was still of great value to the local community over a long period of time.

As with so many former railway lines which have now vanished from the modern world, one wonders what the very distinguished gathering, who on August 6th 1869 watched Mr Henry Martin lay the last brick in the eastern pier of the viaduct at Lewes Road, would say today if they could only see what has happened to the Kemp Town branch line.

08 class 0-6-0 No.D3220 emerging with a train of coal wagons from the northern end of the Kemp Town Tunnel on July 10th 1969. It is hard to believe that what looks very much a rural scene is in fact in the middle of one of the most built-up areas of Brighton. John A.M.Vaughan

Acknowledgements

I would like to thank the following people and organisations for their kind help in compiling information and supplying photographs for this publication: Mr.R.C.Riley, Mr.S.C.Nash, Mr.D.W.Winkworth, Mr.D.Cullum, Mr.J.A.M.Vaughan, Mr.E.Wilmshurst, Mr.P.Hay, Mr.B.R.Hart, Mr.R.M.Casserley (for his and the H.C.Casserley photographs), Mr.J.H.Meredith, Mr.G.Jacobs, Mr.G.R.Croughton, Mr.T.Middlemass, Mr.R.Stumpf, Mr.J.L.Smith of Lens of Sutton, the librarians and staff at Brighton Library, the Public Records Office at Kew, the East Sussex Public Records Office at Lewes, Mr.J.Minnis and members of the Brighton Circle and to all the many people from the Brighton area who contacted me following my request for information in the local papers and radio.

My thanks to my son Paul for reading my text and also to James Christian of Binfield Printers Ltd.

Bibliography

FORGOTTEN RAILWAYS: SOUTH-EAST ENGLAND by H.P.White (David & Charles)
THE RAILWAYS OF SOUTHERN ENGLAND: SECONDARY AND BRANCH LINES by Edwin Course (Batsford)
STROUDLEY AND HIS 'TERRIERS' by Tom Middlemass (Pendragon)
LOCOMOTIVES OF THE L.B.&.S.C.R. Part 1, 2 & 3 by D.L.Bradley (The Railway Correspondence and Travel Society)
THE BRIGHTON TERRIERS by C.J.Binnie (Ravensbourne Press))
SOUTHERN RAILWAY BRANCH LINE TRAINS by R.W.Kidner (Oakwood Press)
RAILWAY MAGAZINE (By Rail to Kemp Town by R.C.Riley. December 1952)
RAILWAY WORLD (The Kemp Town branch by J.M.Tolson. August 1970)

The remains of Lewes Road Station looking towards Kemp Town on December 15th 1962. By this time not only had the footbridge been removed but also the station buildings. Edwin Wilmshurst

'OVER THE ALPS'
on the Watercress Line

*Realising a boyhood dream
in the 21st century*

by
John Richardson

THE OAKWOOD PRESS

© Oakwood Press & John Richardson 2008

British Library Cataloguing in Publication Data
A Record for this book is available from the British Library
ISBN 978 0 85361 683 2

Typeset by Oakwood Graphics.
Repro by PKmediaworks, Cranborne, Dorset.
Printed by Cambrian Printers, Aberystwyth, Ceredigion.

The summit of the 'Alps' - Boyneswood Lane Bridge.   *Author*

Front cover: Rebuilt 'Merchant Navy' class 4-6-2 No. 35005 *Canadian Pacific*, with the author driving, climbs the final quarter mile to the summit early in 2006.   *B. Zehetmayr*

Rear cover, top: Dream come true - the author drives Gresley 'A4' class Pacific No. 60019 *Bittern* up Medstead bank in January 2008.   *www.mattallenphoto.co.uk*

Rear cover bottom: The author on the footplate of Maunsell 'U' class No. 31625 - looking rather warm.   *P. Goodworth*

Published by The Oakwood Press (Usk), P.O. Box 13, Usk, Mon., NP15 1YS.
E-mail: sales@oakwoodpress.co.uk
Website: www.oakwoodpress.co.uk

Contents

	Introduction	4
	Acknowledgements	5
	List of Abbreviations	6
	Glossary	6
Chapter One	Trainspotting	7
Chapter Two	Joining the Railway	17
Chapter Three	Third Man	25
Chapter Four	Experience Gained and Some Weight Lost	37
Chapter Five	*Black Prince*, 'Thomas' and the 'U Boat'	57
Chapter Six	Bulleid Pacifics - the Science Bit	71
Chapter Seven	A Firing Turn on *Swanage*	81
Chapter Eight	Motive Power Miscellany	91
Chapter Nine	Gresley's Masterpiece	107
Chapter Ten	Learner Driver	117
Chapter Eleven	The Other Side of the Footplate	131
Appendix	List of Locomotives fired or driven by the Author	143

The author about to have a drive on *Bodmin* in 2002. The black beret was the favoured headgear of GWR main line firemen at Old Oak Common shed - comparisons with Frank Spencer are not appreciated!   *Author's Collection*

Introduction

With the possible exception of cookery, there have probably been more books written about railways than almost any other subject; so what is likely to be different about this one? Well, in the first place, a great proportion of railway books fall into the nostalgic category - they may be pictorial histories of a certain railway company or branch line, books about particular classes of locomotives and their designers, or otherwise, books of a biographical nature written by former railwaymen. This book is neither, firstly because I have never been a professional railwayman and secondly because it deals with a line that remains in operation today and where large steam locomotives still have to work hard for their living over severe gradients.

The railway in question is that part of the old London & South Western Railway between Alton and Alresford in Hampshire, now known as the Mid-Hants Railway or the 'Watercress Line'. It was nicknamed the 'Alps' in steam days because of the very steep gradients on either side of Medstead summit, which often called for the double-heading of heavy trains.

The book then is a biography dealing with my long love affair with the steam locomotive and particularly my involvement as a volunteer footplateman on the Mid-Hants Railway. Essentially, it is about a little boy who wanted to be an engine driver and who eventually became one. I hope this will appeal to anyone with an interest in steam railways, whether they be armchair enthusiasts who may once have harboured a dream of becoming an engine driver, or others who may already be active members of a preservation group.

To make the book more readable, I have tried to avoid too much in the way of facts and figures and technical detail, apart from the chapter on Bulleid Pacifics. These engines are still the focus of a great deal of argument amongst steam enthusiasts some 60 years after they were introduced and as a qualified engineer myself, I thought I might as well make my contribution to the controversy.

I have included a short glossary and list of abbreviations at the start of the book, but for the most part I have endeavoured to explain a lot of the railway terminology, including some historical background where appropriate, as I come to it in the text, and trust that this will not be found too tedious by those who are already familiar with such things.

I have used the standard notation for writing locomotive wheel arrangements; e.g. a 4-6-2 (also known as a 'Pacific') means it has four small wheels at the front (a bogie) then six large wheels (driving or coupled wheels) and lastly, two more small wheels at the rear (a trailing truck) - the wheels on the tender are not recorded. I have stuck with imperial units throughout, but the only conversions the younger reader may need to know are that 25 mm is slightly less than one inch and 15 psi is slightly more than one bar.

I dedicate the book to my long suffering family, who have had to put up with being disturbed by my getting up at some ungodly hour in the mornings and who still remembered to have a cold beer in the fridge when I returned, grubby and exhausted, in the evenings. Also to driver Bob Cartwright, who remained unfailingly cheerful despite having to put up with me as his fireman for five years, with whom I enjoyed many wonderful days out on the railway 'playing trains' and who taught me so much about railway work in general and in particular, the finer points of firing and driving steam locomotives.

The summit marker board at Boyneswood Lane Bridge.

Author

Acknowledgements

The author would like to say a big thank you to the following people for all the help and encouragement given to me during the years I have worked on the Railway and for assistance in the production of this book, these include the following:

Mick Austen, Geoff Bailey, Norman Batstone, Frank Boait, John Bunch, Mike Burke, Pat Butler, Chris Churm, Alan Coulsell, otherwise known as 'Bubs' (who showed me a few useful tips in the machine shop), Ian Cooper, Norman Cunnington (my first firing instructor), Barry Eden (who was the first person to let me actually drive a steam locomotive), Richard Faithful, John Gibbins, Mick Harris, Keith Hoddy, Clive Holiday, Rosey Jacob, Keith Laughlin, Jim Lawrence, Roger Latch (who gave me very nice shovel), Dave Marsh, Doug Mills, Andrew Netherwood (for teaching a boiler inspector a few more things about boilers!), Mike Pearson, Barry Stratton, Roger Thornton, Tom Turner, Frank Twine (who provides the magnificent permanent way on which we run the trains), the two Dave Wisemans (father & son) and in particular to Bob Cartwright, my good friend and mentor for the past six years.

To Matt Allen, Gwen Cartwright, Rob Forster, Peter Goodworth, Jeremy Hosking, Anne Newman at HIT Entertainment, Keith Stockley, Steve Walters, Tony Wood and Ben Zehetmayr for providing photographs or repro permission for this book.

To Bob Deeth, for never giving up in his efforts at turning all of us amateurs into something roughly resembling professionals.

To Ken Pickering, Dudley Bason and Bob Cartwright for their help in proof-reading the book and for the many useful suggestions and corrections they offered.

To my wife Astrid, for putting up with all the early morning disturbances and for never telling me I should take up stamp collecting or golf instead.

To my two daughters Joanna and Ellen, for help in re-typing some of the manuscript when a computer crash lost a few chapters and for boring themselves silly while proof-reading other parts.

To Dick Hardy for proof-reading the chapter on Bulleid Pacifics and proffering a few suggestions and corrections.

To Mr David Butcher who gave me advice on publication.

To the late L.T.C. Rolt for his book *Red for Danger*, which should be compulsory reading for anyone about to embark upon a railway career and from which I obtained the details of the Abermule and Armagh disasters.

List of Abbreviations

BR	British Railways
GWR	Great Western Railway
HSE	Health & Safety Executive
LBSCR	London Brighton & South Coast Railway
LMS	London Midland & Scottish Railway
LNER	London & North Eastern Railway
LNWR	London & North Western Railway
LSWR	London & South Western Railway
mph	Miles per hour
MHR	Mid-Hants Railway
MR	Midland Railway
psi	Pounds per square inch
SR	Southern Railway
TGV	*Train de Grand Vitesse* – the French high speed train

Glossary

Blower	A device for drawing up the fire - works by squirting a jet of steam up the funnel which induces a partial vacuum in the smokebox, thereby pulling the fire through the tubes.
Clock	The boiler pressure gauge.
Coal pick	Like a small pickaxe - but with a hammer head on one side for breaking up the bigger lumps of coal.
Damper	A moveable flap on the ashpan for regulating the amount of air supplied to the fire.
Dart	A fire iron with a blunt chisel point, used to knock clinker off the fire bars. May be straight or bent - the latter to get in under the firedoor. Also part of the lock which holds the smokebox door closed.
Dummy	A ground signal - usually a white disc with a red band.
Ejector	A device for creating a vacuum for the braking system.
Feeder	The driver's oil can - usually has a long spout and has to be tipped up to get the oil to run out.
Gauge glass	A glass tube mounted in a protective frame on the back of the boiler to display the water level therein - the most important gauge on the engine and usually fitted in pairs in case one breaks.
Injector	A device used to supply water to the boiler.
Paddle	A fire iron with a shovel on the end of a long handle - used to empty ash and clinker out of the firebox.
Pricker	A fire iron with the last foot bent over at right angles - may be used as a rake for levelling the fire or to scrape along the fire bars and around the sides of the firebox when fire cleaning.
Regulator	The handle that makes an engine go - controls the amount of steam supplied to the cylinders.
Reverser	The lever or wheel that controls the valve gear and determines whether the engine runs forward or backwards.
Safety valve	A spring-loaded valve designed to release any excess steam when the pressure reaches the maximum allowed - always two fitted but big engines may have three or four.
Smokebox	The black cylindrical bit at the front of a locomotive boiler - supposed to be airtight except where the chimney pokes through.

Chapter One

Trainspotting

If you drive westwards from Guildford along the A31, it will take you over the Hog's Back, through Farnham and eventually down to Bournemouth. This road has always had pleasant memories for me because driving down it would mean going on holiday to the New Forest or the West Country. About five miles beyond the village of Four Marks on the old road (there is now a by-pass around Alresford), it passes beneath a railway bridge, and although I had driven under it scores of times I had never seen a train cross it. I thought the line must have been one of Dr Beeching's casualties of the early sixties, now long abandoned. One sunny day in 1983 however, as I approached the bridge, I was astonished to see the unmistakeable outline of a Southern 2-6-0 tender engine passing over. The crew gave me a friendly wave, while for my part I was so surprised I nearly went off the road on the bend that follows. A mile or so further on, in the town of Alresford, I spotted a sign for the station and resolved to pay it a visit on our return from holiday.

A week later found me turning into the station car park; a plume of smoke rising from behind the buildings showed that I had struck lucky and that a train was there. I hastily parked the car and walked through onto the platform, to be greeted by the improbable sight of an elderly Drummond 'T9' 4-4-0 at the head of a three-coach train. Some 80 years earlier, these engines were the mainstay of the London & South Western Railway express services, earning the nickname 'Greyhounds' and although I had been a trainspotter for years when I was a boy, I had never seen one before. I had but a scant couple of minutes to admire the engine before departure time, but all the old memories came flooding back - a glimpse of the fire, the ring of the shovel on the firehole as the fireman put on a round of coal and of course that wonderful smell of hot oil and coal smoke that is unique to a steam engine. All too soon, the guard was giving the green flag and blowing his whistle, to be given an answering toot from the engine and then she was puffing sedately away up the line toward Alton and was soon lost to view. I stayed a minute or so longer, listening to the echo of her exhaust beat in the cutting until finally silence reigned again. As I made my way back to my waiting family in the car, I have to confess to feeling a bit of a lump in the throat as I recalled all the happy days I had spent round smoky stations and engine sheds 20 and more years before.

I have always loved steam engines of any kind, whether they be railway locomotives, steam rollers, marine engines or stationary engines in factories, (not many of those around the leafy suburbs of West Wickham in Kent where I was brought up), but railway engines were my favourite. This affection started from about the age of three, when my Dad would sometimes take me to East Croydon station on the Brighton line, to see 'the puffers'. The first clear memory I have from childhood, is of being lifted up onto the footplate of an engine during one of these visits and feeling the heat of the fire.

My Dad was a great tinkerer and was always busy out in the garage making or repairing all sorts of odd bits and pieces. His hobby was photography and he had made nearly all his own darkroom equipment, including a complete enlarger, the body of which was made from a large tin can onto which had been soldered some cooling fins. The enlarging lens came from a pre-war (the first war that is!) plate camera, while the condensing lens, which focused the light from the bulb had been extracted from a naval signalling lamp, which had somehow come into his possession. The whole thing had become the subject of a series of articles in *Hobbies* magazine, which was popular in the 1930s.

Watching and helping my Dad out in the garage cutting metal, drilling holes and soldering bits of tin plate and brass together, became the basis of my interest in things mechanical. This interest was furthered by my elder brother Peter, who was another semi-permanent resident of the garage, where he spent hours and hours overhauling and modifying his various motorbikes. Watching him out there gave me my first experience of seeing an engine taken to bits so I could see how it worked. I can remember one occasion when he wanted to test run the engine of one of his old Triumphs which he had just decoked. The petrol tank was still off the bike, so he had me hold a funnel connected to the carburettor with a rubber tube, while he poured petrol down it from a milk bottle as the engine roared away. It is quite alarming now to dwell on what might have happened had I dropped my end over the open exhaust but all was well.

Actually, motorbikes were one of the few interests of Peter's that I failed to share. I can remember once being taken for a ride on the back of some horrible Aerial contraption with girder forks, to see our sister Jean, who was living in South Godstone at the time. Doing 80 mph down the Caterham by-pass while hanging onto Peter's waist for dear life is one experience I will never forget - and never want to repeat either.

The author, aged four, on board one of his brother Peter's motorcycles.

Author's Collection

One Christmas I was presented with a small Mamod steam engine fired by little blocks of solidified methylated spirits. When the supply of blocks ran out, my Dad and I concocted an alternative from a small paint tin with a pipe soldered into the bottom, which supplied a wick under the boiler with liquid meths, which were a lot cheaper. This engine was one of my favourite toys and I used to spend hours tinkering with it on the kitchen table and trying (mostly unsuccessfully) to rig up belt drives to power some of my other creations that I had made from Meccano, which had been the previous year's Christmas present.

Around that time I was also interested in model aircraft and had a tiny diesel engine for the power plant. The fuel for this came in little square cans with metal spouts sticking out the top. I decided to try and make my own engine, by converting one of these empty cans into a steam turbine (really just a steam windmill) by soldering a couple of brackets on the top of the can and making up a wheel to run on a shaft between them, mounted directly over the spout. The wheel was made from a tin plate disc, around the edge of which I had made about 20 hacksaw cuts in toward the middle. Each blade was then formed by twisting it almost at right angles with a pair of pliers. When I tried it out, I soon found that it didn't produce enough power to drive anything from the shaft but it did spin at an enormous speed and made a very satisfying whirring noise.

One day I had it on the stove in the kitchen and had turned the gas up a bit higher than usual, the speed increased even more but suddenly there was a nasty clunking sound so I turned the gas off in a hurry. The little boiler had been making steam faster than it could get away up the spout and had eventually caused the sides of the can to bulge quite alarmingly. This made me think about what might happen if the steam couldn't get away at all - I couldn't wait to find out!

The first thing required was a more substantial tin can; this came in the shape of a two pound Tate & Lyle golden syrup tin - a quality can if ever there was one. Into this I poured about one inch of water and then took the biggest of Dad's soldering irons, heated it up until the bit showed the correct temperature (gas flames go a nice bright green colour) and soldered the lid down. It was Guy Fawkes night the following day, so I secreted my little device in the middle of the bonfire at the bottom of the garden and awaited events. When the fire was eventually lit, I waited nervously for ages but nothing happened and I wondered if my soldering had failed. Eventually however, there was a spectacular explosion, which exceeded even my wildest expectations - the bonfire was virtually blown to bits and it was a miracle that no-one was hurt by the burning debris. My Dad soon found the remains of the can and there was really no point in denying who was the culprit, so I owned up and was sent inside and had to watch the fireworks from an upstairs window as punishment. This episode did at least teach me to respect the power of steam!

By the time I was seven, I had a bike, and on most evenings if the weather was fair, would cycle down to my local suburban electric line, which I had discovered had one steam train a day. This was a goods train, that arrived around 7.30 pm, behind an old 0-6-0 tender engine (possibly a Wainwright 'C' class from New Cross shed), which spent a quarter of an hour or so shunting the

The author (*left*) trainspotting at Bricklayers Arms shed *circa* 1959.   *Author's Collection*

coal yard at West Wickham station, before rumbling off down the line to do the same at Hayes, which was the terminus. In those pre-central heating days, virtually every station had a similar small coal yard and they were all quite busy.

I was also allowed to go by myself on the bus to East Croydon, where there was still quite a lot of steam to be seen - mostly Southern 2-6-0s of the 'U' and 'N' classes and British Railways (BR) Standard 2-6-4 tank engines. I was particularly impressed by the way northbound trains would come bursting under the road bridge at the country end of the station and then hurtle down the platform, sending the newspapers flying from unwary hands before coming gently to a stand at the far end of platform 4, in order to take water from the column. This was driving skill of the highest order, although it was not until I finally got to have a go myself, 40-odd years later that I realised it.

The footbridge spanning the far end of the platforms at Bromley South was another favourite haunt and being on the main line to the Kent coast, had a much wider variety of motive power to be seen. The highlight of the day was to see the 'Golden Arrow' express run through, with its long rake of chocolate and cream Pullman coaches, hauled by a sparkling clean 'Merchant Navy' or 'Britannia' Pacific, carrying the famous golden arrow motifs on the smokebox door and on the sides of the boiler, together with the British and French flags over the buffers.

Before much longer, all my pocket money was being spent on bus and train fares to ever more distant locations, in my quest to see as many different engines as possible. Two shillings would buy a return ticket from West Wickham to Charing Cross, and from there, a few pence more on the tube would get me to all the other great London stations and engine sheds. By the time I was 10 years old, I knew my way around the capital better than I do now. My trips were not just confined to London either; Reading, Tonbridge, Redhill and Hitchin were just some of the places I visited when funds would allow it. Hitchin, about 30 miles north of Kings Cross, on the East Coast main line, was a wonderful place to see engines at speed. There were four tracks here - the slow lines through the platforms with the up and down fast lines in between. At the north end of the platforms there were telegraph repeater instruments, which indicated 'line clear' or 'train approaching' for the four running lines, to let the station staff know if it was safe to cross the tracks - also very handy for us trainspotters. The warning was very necessary, because the main line expresses, invariably with a Pacific at the head, would tear through the station at speeds well up into the eighties, or possibly even more.

Maunsell 'N' class 2-6-0 No. 31411 at Redhill engine shed in January 1965.
Provenance Unknown

A young trainspotter looks on as Peppercorn 'A1' class Pacific No. 60136 *Alzacar* arrives at Kings Cross with the 9.40 am from Newcastle on 18th August, 1957.　　*R.A. Panting*

If things were quiet, we could try and bunk round the shed, which was situated alongside the London end of the up platform. This mostly contained a few 'N2' class 0-6-2 tank engines for the local stopping trains and some 0-6-0 goods engines. I was surprised one day however, to find a solitary 'A3' Pacific standing in the yard, looking rather like a Masai warrior surrounded by pigmies. I imagine it had broken down on a southbound express and had been turned into the shed for repair - or maybe even to just get it out of the way. It is interesting to speculate what motive power Hitchin shed might have provided to take the train on to Kings Cross!

On one of these trips to Hitchin, I was waiting at Kings Cross for the engine to back down onto the train and was amazed when it turned out to be an 'A4' Pacific – and not just any old 'A4' either; it was No. 60022 *Mallard* - the world's fastest steam locomotive. With a determined driver and an equally valiant fireman, this engine had run at 126 mph in 1938, during a brake testing run, to take the world record for steam traction - a record which is now unlikely ever to be broken. The engine was in pristine condition and was doing a running-in turn after overhaul in Doncaster works - and, I regret to say, did not travel at much more than 30 mph all the way to Hitchin!

I have always felt it rather incongruous that the world's fastest steam locomotive should be named after a duck, and that the title would have sat more regally on one of the other engines of the class (34 were built) - No. 60014 *Quicksilver* perhaps, or No. 60018 *Sparrowhawk*, which at least is pretty fast sort of bird. On the other hand, I suppose *Mallard* is better than *Walter K. Whigham* (60028), whoever he was!

For the return journey, the train came in five minutes late behind a filthy dirty 'A2' Pacific, No. 60506 *Wolf of Badenoch*, one of Edward Thompson's rebuilds of the Gresley 'P2' class 2-8-2. I just had time to speak to the driver before departure and told him I had come up behind *Mallard* and how dismally slow it had been. He looked across at his fireman and remarked 'We had better see what this old girl can do then' and blew his whistle, which sent me scurrying back into the first coach. Right from the outset, it was clear that this driver meant business and the speed mounted rapidly, I was timing the train on my wristwatch, which had a sweep second hand. There were two ways of doing it: you could either watch the quarter mile posts as they flashed past, or else count 22 rail joints which was the same distance. The time taken, divided into 900 gave the speed in miles per hour. As my timings got down to 10 seconds (90 mph), I was getting more and more excited - would we reach the magic 100? In the end we didn't quite, but my timings were certainly nearer the required 9 seconds than 10, so I reckon the speed was in the high 90s - certainly the fastest I ever went behind a steam engine.

We eventually arrived back in Kings Cross having caught up several of the lost minutes and I walked down to see the engine, now simmering quietly at the buffer stops, with no indication of the furious run that had just taken place. I was invited up onto the footplate and had a look in that cavernous firebox, to find that the fire had died down to just a red mass, with hardly a flame to be seen. I reckoned the fireman must have packed up shovelling somewhere back around Potters Bar; anyway, he was now sitting with his feet up, reading the paper and looking quite relaxed. I thanked the driver for such a good run and was offered a cheese sandwich in return, which was typical of the kindness shown by many engine crews in those days.

Occasionally I ventured even further afield; the most memorable trip being to Doncaster on an Ian Allan trainspotters' excursion. For motive power we had a pair of venerable 4-4-0s, one was the Great Western *City of Truro*, reputedly the first engine ever to achieve 100 mph, the other being the preserved Midland Compound No. 1000. On our arrival at Doncaster we had a conducted tour of the locomotive works, which I found quite enthralling, even though there were already a few diesel engines to be seen amongst the steamers. On the return journey, much to my chagrin, for I was a fervent Great Western fan in those days and didn't have a good word to say about any Midland engine, *City of Truro* had to come off the train in disgrace with a hot axlebox. Despite my disappointment, I had to admire the ensuing performance of the Midland Compound, which put up a terrific effort and got us back to Kings Cross without losing any more time. This ability to rise to the occasion and pull off an extraordinary feat of haulage, is I think one of the most appealing features of steam traction. With a diesel or electric locomotive you can put the power handle over to maximum and there is nothing more to be done, whereas with steam, the right combination of driver, fireman and locomotive can sometimes produce results that on paper would look impossible.

The summer holidays also provided the opportunity for some longer railway journeys. One year I was sent to a summer camp in North Cornwall for a week, which gave me the chance of travelling down on the best train of the day: the 'Atlantic Coast Express' from Waterloo. Nine Elms shed provided a reasonably smart 'Merchant Navy' Pacific for this duty - No. 35018 *British India Line*, I seem to recall. As we swept through Clapham Junction, it made a pleasant change to actually be on the train, instead of standing on the platform and swivelling round to watch it run past, as I had done many times before. The highlight of the journey was the sprint down the bank from Axminster and through Seaton Junction, which lies in a dip at the foot of two inclines. Our crew had *British India Line* worked up to more than 90 mph as we hurtled through the station, with the driver hanging on the whistle before roaring away on the climb up to Honiton. Exeter was reached on time but after this, things went downhill. Our 'Merchant Navy' came off and was replaced by an un-rebuilt and unremembered 'Battle of Britain' 4-6-2, of grubby appearance and slothful performance. It ambled all round the north side of Dartmoor and down into Cornwall, detaching coaches here and there for the various other branch lines leading up to the coast, before reaching Wadebridge where I got off, some 30 minutes late.

Another year, I went to stay with a boy from Birmingham, who my family had met up with on a previous holiday and had become friends with. They suggested I travel up from Euston to New Street station in Birmingham but I soon managed to talk them out of that idea. There was only one way to Birmingham for me and that was from Paddington to Snow Hill on the 10.10 am 'Cambrian Coast Express', which was timed at just under two hours for the 115 miles. This train was often provided with a 'King' class 4-6-0 for motive power and on the day I went, I was lucky enough to find No. 6000 *King George V* at its head. This was in really superb condition with sparkling green paintwork, while the copper-capped chimney and all the brasswork (the Great Western Railway (GWR) always had a lot of that) were absolutely gleaming. She was still carrying the brass bell on the buffer beam, which had been presented to her when she visited America in 1927 for some trade fair. This particular engine also gave me a very exciting journey and I recorded another top speed in the 90s.

When you consider that I was only around nine years old when I first started these wanderings, the amount of freedom I was allowed by my parents must seem astonishing to young people today - indeed I certainly never allowed my own children to wander around on their own like I did as a boy. I daresay there were paedophiles and child murderers around in those days too, but we never seemed to hear about them and society in general seemed to be a safer place. Even so, there were a couple of incidents that stand out in my mind that would have given my poor mother heart failure if she had ever found out and would certainly have led to a ban on my unsupervised wanderings.

The first of these occurred at Old Oak Common shed in north-west London, which served the former Great Western lines out of Paddington. This great shed was always a favourite of mine, mainly because it was very easy to get into and once inside, nobody ever threw me out. It contained four massive turntables in the main building, each with numerous shiny Western engines stabled around it - 'Kings', 'Castles' and 'Halls' were there in abundance, together with loads of the smaller suburban 2-6-2 tank engines and 0-6-0 Pannier tanks. On this occasion I was standing just inside one of the entrance doors, with a foot on the rail of one of the turntable roads. I was so engrossed in looking round at the engines inside that I failed to notice another creeping up behind me. I was standing in the gloom on the fireman's side of the engine and would have been quite invisible to the driver coming in from the bright sunshine outside. If I

'Castle' class 4-6-0 No. 5053 *Earl Cairns* and BR Standard '9F' class 2-10-0 No. 92004 in Old Oak Common roundhouse on 30th April, 1960.   *J. L. Stevenson*

hadn't felt a slight movement of the rail under my foot as the engine approached, I would have been run down. As it was, the engine was only about six feet away when I turned round and saw it – a very lucky escape! The locomotive in question was No. 7029 *Clun Castle*, one of the fortunate few that escaped the gas torch in the breaker's yard.

   The second incident, although it did not involve any near misses, would still be enough to give apoplexy to any Health and Safety officer of today. It involved a visit to Kings Cross shed, which was as difficult to get into as Old Oak Common was easy - my previous two attempts had ended up by my being booted out by the foreman before I had even seen an engine. I have to say that this was an uncommon reaction, as nearly all the other railwaymen I met showed remarkable tolerance to scruffy urchins such as myself and would often invite us up onto the footplate and chat to us - occasionally even offering a drink of stewed tea from their cans; I only tried this once - quite horrible! On the day in question, I was actually at St Pancras station, which of course is right next door to Kings Cross on the Euston Road. I was chatting to another boy I had met and happened to mention my lack of success with Kings Cross shed, to which he replied that he would get me in there in return for one of my sandwiches. This seemed like a reasonable deal, so I handed over the butty and trotted along behind my guide who took me over to the Kings Cross side of the station and down to the end of the far platform. Then he had a quick look round to make sure we were not being observed by the station staff, before marching straight off the end of the platform and down the tracks! After a short distance we veered off to the right into the gasworks, where we ducked and dived between the pipes and retorts to avoid detection, before arriving in a shunting yard. Here we had to wend our way through several lines of wagons, some of which were moving, before reaching the far side. After a gap of some 40 years, my memory is a bit hazy about the final leg of the journey but I seem to remember it involved climbing down from some sort of viaduct before finally arriving in

Kings Cross shed yard. Our triumph only lasted about 10 minutes, before we were spotted and turfed out into the street, but this was not before we had seen a good many of the engines in residence.

It seems that all good things come to an end and by 1960 it was clear that steam was doomed, along with my youthful dream of becoming an engine driver. The lists of engines withdrawn from service which appeared each month in *Trains Illustrated* magazine became longer and longer, while those that remained looked more and more dirty and uncared for. When I first saw the 'Cornish Riviera' express pull out of Paddington behind a diesel, trainspotting ceased to be of much interest, so my spare time could now be devoted to my other hobbies, which included fishing and building model aircraft.

In 1964 I left school and joined the Merchant Navy as an Engineer Cadet. Here at least there was still plenty of steam about, albeit mostly in the shape of steam turbines and water tube boilers. During my apprenticeship however, I was lucky enough to do one five month trip on a coastal tanker propelled by an 'up and downer' (steam reciprocating engine), and in fact it was not until 1976 that I first served on a motor vessel. I had got married in 1974, and by the time our first child was born five years later, I had already given up the deep sea life and transferred to the cross-channel ferries, working out of Dover and Folkestone, which is where I was in 1983, when this chapter begins.

Despite my long lasting affection for the steam locomotive, I had never really considered joining a railway preservation society. There were two main reasons for this: firstly I imagined that it would probably mean years of shed work before my turn came up for footplate duties and secondly, the only railway within easy reach from my home in Canterbury was the Kent & East Sussex Railway, which was a small engine branch line starting from Tenterden, some 10 miles south-west of Ashford. One of my fellow Chief Engineers on the ferries was a driver there and kindly arranged for me to have a footplate ride over the line. Although I enjoyed it very much, the only real interest from the driving and firing point of view was the short but steep bank from Rolvenden up to Tenterden Town and I feared that I might soon become bored with it. Also, I have always found tank engine footplates to be horribly cramped - no room for visitors and with hot pipes all over the place to burn the unwary. Although I enjoy the branch line atmosphere, it has always been big engines working hard that have given me the biggest thrill.

Shortly after this, I happened to meet Michael Draper, who was then in charge of the Severn Valley Railway, while I was Chief Engineer on a ferry called the *Lion*. In return for a conducted tour of the bridge and engine room of the ship, he arranged for me to have a footplate ride over his railway, when we went on holiday to Shropshire later that year. The motive power on this occasion was an Ivatt 2-6-0 tender engine, unkindly nicknamed the 'flying pig'. With a 10-coach train, the engine had to be worked quite hard - leaving Bridgnorth, I can remember the regulator being opened fully as soon as we were off the end of the platform. This was a much more exciting prospect, but the Severn Valley was more than 200 miles away. However, I had acquired an Aveling & Porter steam roller to play with and was building a model 5 inch gauge 'Britannia' Pacific, so my steam interests were at least partly satisfied.

Chapter Two

Joining the Railway

In 1993, I was employed as a Chief Engineer on the Seacat services, working either the Dover-Calais or the Folkestone-Boulogne routes. These high speed catamarans, which could carry around 70 cars, were an engineer's nightmare when they first appeared, and had I kept a diary of all the events that took place in 1992 and 1993, I would have had enough material for a very damning book about them. Engine failures, hydraulic failures and electrical black-outs were occurring almost every day during one period and I even had a crankcase explosion on a main engine on one occasion. This had been caused by a bearing failure on a turbocharger, where a piece of red hot shrapnel from the destroyed bearing had gone back down the oil return pipe into the engine sump and had ignited the oil vapour therein. Fortunately, I had been at my station on the bridge at the time and had noticed the engine revs beginning to drop, which gave time to warn the Captain to shut the engine down. This he did very promptly, but not before the bang, which caused all the explosion doors on the engine to open and let out tremendous gusts of flame and smoke (we could see all this on the engine room closed circuit TV) - luckily, there was nobody in the engine room at the time and so not much damage occurred, apart from to the turbocharger, which was a write-off.

What with all the technical problems and a worry that the owners (Sea Containers) might pull the plug and cut their losses, I started to cast around for something else to do. I had a double-barrelled Chief's ticket (1st class Steam & Motor Certificate) and not much else. I began scouring the appointment pages in the papers and after a few months spotted an advert for a boiler inspector with a leading insurance company. This sounded right up my street, so I applied immediately and got the job, despite being a year older than the preferred upper age limit of 45.

There was just one rather large problem: I had to move down to Surrey to work the area I had been given, while my wife remained in Kent with the children, because they were settled in good schools and we did not want to disrupt their education. This meant that after I had finished my week's work, I would go back to Canterbury on the Friday night, and return to Cranleigh, where we had bought another house, on the Monday morning; alternatively, my family would come down to me for the weekend. Initially, this was a great strain, especially for my wife, but we soon got used to it, and the fact that we are still together after more than 30 years of marriage must say something. In fact, we soon became very fond of the village of Cranleigh and all the beautiful countryside around it, where we could take the dogs for walks. There was one other positive factor - Cranleigh was only about 45 minutes away from the Mid-Hants Railway (MHR) at Ropley.

My company did all the boiler inspections for the Railway, although it was not actually on my patch. However, I soon got to know Ian Farrance, whose area it was and persuaded him to take me along for a visit, when he next went there to carry out an inspection. When the day came, I met Ian at Ropley, which is on the A31 a couple of miles west of Four Marks and where the locomotive department of the Mid–Hants Railway is based. Here, I assisted Ian with a cold examination of the boiler of a Bulleid Pacific - No. 34105 *Swanage*.

After my colleague had finished, I remained and had a chat with Andrew Netherwood, who was charge of the boiler department there. Andrew was also an ex-marine engineer, so we hit it off right from the start and when he learned of my steam interests, he very kindly arranged for me to have a footplate ride to Alton and back on No. 30506, which was an 'S15' class 4-6-0 tender engine - really just like a 'King Arthur' but with smaller wheels. I did not take notes of this trip and cannot remember many details, except to notice the severity of the line. Leaving Alton on the return journey, we were on full regulator and 45 per cent cut-off as soon as we cleared the points leading out of the station, while the noise from the chimney was quite fearsome and sounded more Great Western than Southern (Great Western engines were renowned for their very sharp exhaust beats).

The term cut-off, which crops up occasionally in this narrative, means the percentage of the piston stroke during which steam is admitted to the cylinders and can be varied by the driver from zero (this is called mid-gear) to about 75 per cent (full gear) in both forward and reverse directions. Full gear is used to obtain maximum torque when starting off and this is then reduced progressively as the train gathers speed, to take advantage of the expansive properties of the steam, thereby giving more economical running. This process is called 'notching up' and comes about because a lot of older engines had a big

Urie 'S15' class 4-6-0 in original livery takes water at Ropley. During all my time on the railway it was painted in BR lined black and numbered 30506.   *P. Goodworth*

reversing lever operating in a quadrant with numerous notches cut in it, into which the pawl of a ratchet could be engaged, in order to fix the lever in the desired position. Most small tank engines and goods engines still use a lever but all the bigger express locomotives have a screw reverse instead, with a big wheel to operate it - many of the younger children ask if this is the steering wheel when they visit the footplate! How much the driver 'notches up' determines how much power the engine will produce (and also how much coal the fireman has to shovel!) A large passenger engine would normally be worked in the 15 to 25 per cent range when running on the level, while 35 to 40 per cent would be sufficient to climb most main line gradients.

During my trip on 30506, I remarked to the driver on how hard I thought the engine was being worked as we left Alton, to which he replied that it would be even harder soon, as we were only on the 1 in 100 at that point and there were nearly three miles of 1 in 60 still to come! For those readers who can only think of hills in terms of road gradients, where anything easier than 1 in 10 is hardly worth a mention, I would point out that 1 in 60 on a railway is pretty steep. Your car would easily climb this sort of hill fully laden in top gear but now imagine you were having to tow three or four similar cars behind you - you would probably guess that it would not be long before you were struggling along in second gear. By way of a comparison, probably the best known gradient of the steam age was Shap incline, on the West Coast main line to Scotland, which although much longer than anything on the Mid-Hants, is only 1 in 75 on the steepest section.

My new job had not turned out to be as interesting as I imagined - I had the occasional traction engine or steam roller to look at but the bulk of the work consisted of examining rusty air receivers in garages and factories, or central heating boilers in office buildings. There was one call, however, that I always looked forward to, which was to inspect the boiler of a steam launch, which was moored on the Thames at Kingston. The owner, Dr Slee and his charming wife, always looked after me very well on these occasions. The builder of the boiler was in attendance to strip down any of the parts that I needed to see and when the cold examination was complete, would then reassemble it. Then we would light the fire in order to carry out the steam test. This would take the form of a cruise down the river for an hour or so - ostensibly to test the safety valves and water feed arrangements but in reality, just to enjoy the ride. Finally, I would be invited back to a pleasant lunch on the terrace of their flat overlooking the river - and I actually got paid for this!

The real benefit of the job, however, was that to a large extent I could pick and choose the hours I worked; providing that I achieved the required number of inspections every week, my boss was satisfied. This meant, that if I chose, I could start work early and finish my inspections by lunchtime, then I could spend the best part of the afternoon at the Railway, before returning home to write up all my inspection reports on the computer in the evening. So it was, that after my footplate ride on the 'S15', I became a regular volunteer in the locomotive department at Ropley, where my fitting and machining skills could be put to good use. In time, my dogs, who used to travel everywhere with me, got to know Ropley station yard pretty well, but they were always very patient because they knew that a nice walk would be forthcoming on the way home.

This would quite often be to the top of Pitch Hill, near Ewhurst, which although not quite so high as nearby Leith Hill, has in my opinion one of the finest views in Surrey, extending almost to the south coast on a clear day.

During this period I worked on all manner of bits and pieces, as directed by Frank Boait, who was the mechanical boss, or Andrew on the boilers. I was amazed by the versatility and professionalism of everyone I met in the loco department - both the paid staff and the volunteers. Piston rings were machined, axleboxes re-metalled, superheater elements manufactured and awkward bits of boiler cladding beaten up from sheet steel using nothing much more than a few hand hammers and dollies - virtually nothing is bought in except the materials. As the machining work is all carried out on a motley collection of second-hand lathes, borers and milling machines, some of which are at least half a century old, this makes their achievements all the more remarkable.

The locomotive department at Ropley consists of a large prefabricated hut opposite the station buildings, somewhat grandiosely named 'Ropley Manor'. This contains the offices, toilets and mess rooms. Walking down from here toward the loco yard, brings you to the shed. Upon entering this through a side door, the machine shop is to be found on the left, with most of the remaining area taken up with the three tracks (always called roads in railway parlance) leading out into the yard. The far road has a full length inspection pit and is where most

Peckett 0-4-0 saddle tank 'Percy' in Ropley yard. The gentleman alongside is mechanical foreman Frank Boait - looking rather glum because 'Percy' has just failed with leaking tubes.   *Author/© 2008 Gullane (Thomas) Ltd*

of the fitting and assembly work is done on the engines. The middle road at that time was occupied by the remains of No. 34016 *Bodmin*, another Bulleid Pacific, this one being of the rebuilt variety, which are minus the streamlined boiler cladding and plus the outside Walschaerts valve gear. The remaining road is where coaches and locomotives are brought in for preparation and painting.

Out in the yard, the three roads continue for about 100 yards before coming together by the water column and then run onto the outside pit road, which, as the name implies has an inspection pit running down part of it. From the pit road there is a turn out onto the running line in the down direction, controlled by a ground signal (always referred to in the trade as a 'dummy'). Dummies are used to control shunting movements and come in two main types: most consist of a white disc with a red band across the middle which is horizontal when at danger and turned through 45 degrees when cleared to pass. This particular one however, is black with a yellow band and is known as a permissive dummy - it can be passed at danger providing the movement is along the pit road, but has to be cleared before a movement is made out onto the running line. The pit road is quite lengthy and continues up beyond an overbridge in the Medstead direction for about a quarter of a mile in total. This end is crammed with dead engines and other rolling stock awaiting their turn in the repair queue. Going down the other way, it runs the full length of the shed and nearly into the station car park. The wheeldrop is installed halfway down it alongside the shed wall. This wheeldrop originally came from Bricklayers Arms shed in South London and was a major engineering feat to restore and install. Although questions were asked at the time about the wisdom of spending the money on this piece of equipment, it must have paid for itself many times over subsequently, because the Railway no longer has to send engines away by road every time they need work on the wheels or axleboxes - this usually had to be done at Tyseley near Birmingham and cost several thousand pounds each way in road haulage fees.

Between the water column and the overbridge, some 2,000 tons of chalk have been excavated from what was originally the cutting flanking the side of the line: this made the space available for a new running shed to be erected. The result is that at last some of the lesser repairs (as opposed to complete rebuilds) can be done under cover. At present it has two roads laid and the remaining space is taken up by the boiler department. Also on this side of the yard are the coal store which is enclosed by a wall made up of old railway sleepers and the oil and wood stores.

The main thrust of the workshop effort when I joined the railway, was the rebuilding of No. 31625, a Southern 'U' class 2-6-0 tender engine, which had been rescued from Barry scrapyard. I made or overhauled quite a few odd bits and pieces for this engine, including lubricator fittings, various bushes for the valve gear and the reversing shaft clutch valve, which can be used by the driver to lock the shaft in the desired position and prevents kickback from the valve gear from being transmitted to the reversing screw in the cab. I also assisted with running repairs to locomotives in the yard when required and can well remember my first encounter with Mr Bulleid's horrible inside valve gear on *Swanage* - but more of this in a later chapter.

One of the jobs I always enjoyed was riveting, despite the ear splitting racket that accompanied it. The rivets had to be heated until they were a bright yellow colour - much more and they would start to burn, any less and they might cool too quickly and go hard before the head had been hammered down. When the rivet was judged to be at the correct temperature, it was picked up with tongs and inserted through the hole. Then one man (the holder up) would apply the shaped dolly to the pre-formed head of the rivet, while another, working on the other side, applied the pneumatic riveting gun and hammered down the protruding stem, hopefully finishing up with a neat hemisphere to match the one at the opposite end. All this had to be done at the double, because the rivets were impossible to work once they had cooled below dull red. The rivet length was also quite critical because if it was too short, the formed head would be undersized and miss-shaped; if it was too long, then the extra metal would extrude from around the base of the head like a ragged washer during the hammering down process and would have to be trimmed off afterwards. If any of the finished rivets did not measure up to Andrew or Frank's exacting standards, they would have to be burnt out using an oxy-acetylene torch (known in the trade as a 'gas axe') and done again. We would always experiment with one rivet first, and having found the correct length, all the others would be hacksawed down to the same size - a somewhat arm aching job if there were a lot to do.

Occasionally, when working in the shed, I would hear the faint rumble as a train arrived and would wander out into the yard to watch it depart for Alton. It was amazing how many other people would find some excuse to do the same thing; even though they might have witnessed the spectacle scores of times before, the true steam fan would never tire of it. We gawpers would collect outside the shed and critically observe the departing train - would the driver get away without wheel slip, was there too much smoke or any blowing off at the safety valves? Finally, the train would disappear under the bridge and we would all go back to work.

On one of these forays into the yard, I was surprised to see the familiar outlines of a Great Western 'Castle' class locomotive parked down by the coal heap. When I walked down for a closer look and the number plate came into view, I was even more surprised, for it was none other than No. 7029 *Clun Castle*, which had nearly run me down almost 40 years previously. I was particularly pleased that this one had survived the cutting torch - it was rather like making up with an estranged family member you hadn't spoken to for decades. I climbed up on the footplate and began to enthuse about her to Andrew and Frank who were also there but found they were by no means as happy to see her as I was - she had a leaking firebox and had developed some mechanical faults as well, since arriving on our line.

This was quite a common occurrence with visiting engines, which may have performed quite happily over their own relatively level track for months without trouble. When they got to our line, however, and suddenly had to do some really hard work, any latent defects soon showed up and had to be repaired by us - hence Andrew and Frank's glum faces. The first thing to go was quite often the deflector plate, which fits in the top half of the firehole door and is designed to direct the incoming air down into the body of the fire, rather than have it whistle straight over the brick arch and down the tubes. With our white hot fires, these would usually only last a few trips before burning away or drooping down at the front, so that it became difficult to throw the coal past them. They could also become such a poor fit in the firehole that they could become dislodged and prevent the firedoor from being closed. When they got to this stage, Dave Sibley, who was another one of the full time staff, would be called upon to roll up another one out of some extra heavy plate.

The boilers in particular take a terrible beating on the Mid-Hants, where you need as much steam as you can get on one half of each trip and then hardly anything for the remainder, so leaking tubes and stays are quite common. On the mechanical side, there are hot bearings, knocking axleboxes, blown piston rod glands and broken springs, to name a few of the more common ailments.

All this wear and tear is hardly surprising, when you consider that a typical day's duty for an engine is three or four round trips of 20 miles each, plus a bit of light engine mileage to and from Alresford or Alton. Out of this, nearly a half is climbing at gradients of between 1 in 60 and 1 in 100. This makes it one of the toughest standard gauge preserved lines in the country from the operational point of view and it is little wonder that the engines need a lot of maintenance. Naturally, what goes up has to come down, so that on all the descents the brakes are being used nearly continuously on both engines and coaching stock, so fitting new brake blocks is another regular chore.

Much as I enjoyed my work in the shed, I was itching to get out on the footplate again and asked Frank how to join a crew, which on the Mid-Hants consists of three men - driver, fireman and third man (or trainee fireman). To progress from cleaner to fireman, depended purely on your ability to do the job and a basic knowledge of the rules and safety procedures. One day you would find yourself out with Bob Deeth, the footplate inspector (now the MHR locomotive superintendent), who would observe your efforts while you fired the engine for a round trip and if you passed muster, you would be put on a crew as fireman when a vacancy occurred. From fireman to driver was much the same, consisting of carrying out a driving turn (including the engine preparation) under Bob's eagle eye but with a much stiffer written exam to pass beforehand. Bob was a former main line driver on the Southern Region during the final years of steam and had quite a reputation for fast running - he had probably accrued more footplate turns during his career than all the rest of us volunteers put together.

This was different from the old railway system, where a crew comprised of just the driver and fireman and you started your career as an engine cleaner, seldom getting the chance to go out on the road. You had to wait your turn, possibly many years before being called for firing duties, then many more before you could take the driving examination. Even then, always assuming you passed the exam, you would not get a driving job straight away and would be classed as a passed fireman (fireman passed for driving duties), until your seniority was sufficient to give you the coveted position at last.

There are about 26 set crews on the Mid-Hants and a roster is posted for all the weekend and bank holiday turns. For the mid-week services, a notice is posted calling for volunteers and any of the regular drivers or firemen can put their names down for these, on a first come, first served basis. The third man positions however were open to anyone in the loco department, providing Bob Deeth had given his approval, so all I had to do was wait for a space on the volunteer sheet and put my name down for it, which I duly did.

Ropley yard with 'Thomas' and 'Douglas' in front and 'James', Nos. 34016, 41312 and 92212 behind. 'Douglas' is actually another 'J94' tank engine with tanks removed and a tender added.
Gwen Cartwright/© 2008 Gullane (Thomas) Ltd

'J94' class 0-6-0 'Douglas' departs Ropley - blowing steam from all conceivable orifices!
R. Forster/© 2008 Gullane (Thomas) Ltd

Chapter Three

Third Man

My first trip as third man was in October 1994 and coincided with the autumn 'Thomas the Tank Engine' week. These 'Thomas' events are very important to the Railway because they always attract large numbers of families with children and are by far the most valuable fund raising events of the year. It is amazing to think that these stories about a little blue engine with a smiling face, which were written by a country clergyman for his son, should still have an enduring fascination for young children today. Indeed, they are so popular that most preserved railways organize similar events - and we all have to pay a certain amount of the proceeds in royalties, because anything to do with 'Thomas' is strictly copyright.

Our particular 'Thomas' is in fact a 'J94' 0-6-0 saddle tank locomotive, which was converted some years ago with side tanks, wheel splashers and a modified coal bunker to conform as closely as possible to the appearance of 'Thomas' in the books.

Another 'J94' has been turned into 'Douglas' by removing the tanks altogether and adding a separate tender. On the Mid-Hants we also have 'James the Red Engine', in the shape of No. 31874, a Southern 'N' class 2-6-0 painted in the appropriate colours and which was my engine for the day. Such is the importance to the railway of these 'Thomas' events, that when No. 31874 had to be withdrawn from service due to firebox problems, 'U' class No. 31625, which is almost identical in appearance was immediately painted red to take its place.

The railway took a good deal of criticism in the railway press for repainting No. 31874, because they said it was the only 'N' class in preservation and should be maintained in original condition. I am afraid I have no sympathy with this point of view. In the first place, without the money brought in by all the families at these 'Thomas' events, the Mid-Hants and quite a lot of other preserved lines would probably fold up, and then there would be no steam at all. Secondly, enthusiasts and photographers (and before I became an active volunteer I would have had to include myself in that category), do not actually contribute very much money to the steam preservation movement and seem happy enough to simply grab a good vantage point from which to take their pictures, rather than buy a ticket and ride a train. Finally, if just a handful of the children who come along to these events to see 'Thomas' and his friends become volunteers themselves when they grow older, it will give the railway preservation movement at least a sporting chance of lasting another generation or two. Having said all that, I am very glad that the Revd Awdry, who wrote the books, did not decide that 'Thomas' should be pink with yellow stripes!

I shall describe my first day out on the footplate in some detail, which will make the following chapters easier to understand and will also I hope, evoke the reality of what it is like to be a locomotive fireman and the duties involved in engine preparation, running and disposal.

When the day finally arrived for my first turn, the alarm clock jolted me awake at 4.45 am, which left me just enough time to grab a piece of toast and a cup of coffee before heading off over the Hog's Back and down the A31 to Ropley. I arrived at the 'Manor' at 6 am, and signed the attendance sheet, putting a tick in the footplate duties column for the first time. The fireman's name was Norman Cunnington, who was a local policeman when he wasn't working on the railway. Norman collected the shed key and we made our way down the cinder track and let ourselves in through the side door; the gloomy interior made the remains of *Bodmin* on the middle road appear even more massive than usual. Norman stepped over to a panel on the wall and threw about 20 switches which slowly brought the mercury vapour interior lights to life and restored everything to its normal perspective.

My first job was to collect two bundles of rags - one clean and one dirty, together with a few pints of paraffin in a bucket for lighting up and cleaning, after which I trotted along behind Norman to the other end of the shed, where we let ourselves out into the yard.

We found our steed over the pit and climbed aboard. Norman immediately fired a question at me, 'What do we always check first before we light the fire?' As a marine engineer, I knew the answer to that one at least, which is of course to open the water gauges and check the water level in the boiler. Having ascertained that we did indeed have a sufficient quantity of the vital fluid - in this case about half a glass, we could proceed to the next stage, which was to dispose of the remains of the previous day's fire. Norman gave me a large iron bar which fitted in a socket by the rear wheels and opened a drop door on the ashpan, which allowed all the ashes to drop into the pit. Back on the footplate, the same bar, together with large quantities of muscle power, had to be heaved back and forth to operate the rocking grate mechanism, which up-ended each individual grate finger and dropped what was left on the firebars through as well. Having done this, any ash that remained around the edges, together with any clinker on the firebars, was cleared away with the various fire irons. Finally the firebars were locked back to the level position and the ashpan door closed.

Having dealt with this end of the boiler, we now turned our attention to the front. First of all, we required a large spanner to undo the six lugs that secured the smokebox door, which then allowed it to be swung open about 90 degrees, where it was stopped by a chain. We were checking that there were no obvious leaks from the tubes or wash-out plugs, that the blast pipe cap, blower pipe and spark arrestor grids were all secure and that the previous crew had made at least a half decent job of clearing out the char (smokebox ash). Providing the bottom rows of tubes were not obstructed and the heap at the front had been removed, it was good enough and we could shut the door again.

Now that all the dust had settled in the firebox, we could stick our head through the firehole and have a good look round, again checking for leaking tubes and stays and that the brick arch was intact. The fusible plugs were carefully scrutinised - any signs of a leak at these and the engine would be deemed a failure and would have to be allowed to cool right down, before Andrew (the boilermaker) could get in and fit a new one. On this occasion, apart from a few weeping stays at the firebox sides which weren't considered to be serious, all was well, so we could light the fire.

For this purpose we used old wooden pallets, suitably smashed up, a supply of which had been kindly stacked in the corner of the cab by the previous crew. First of all, Norman shovelled in a layer of coal to cover the grate, then the wood got a splash or two of paraffin before being thrown down under the brick arch; this was followed by the dirty rags also soaked in paraffin and finally a few more shovels of coal were spread over the top of the heap. One last piece of rag was placed on the shovel and lit with a match; when it was burning well, Norman carefully threw it down the firebox to light our little bonfire and the firedoors could be closed. Tendrils of smoke curled out from around the doors and started to deposit a layer of soot over the cab fittings above, but there was nothing we could do about this until there was about 15 psi on the clock (steam pressure gauge) and we could open the blower to draw the fire through. Today, the needle was just off the stop at around 5 psi, which was not enough to do any good.

Even though we had now lit the fire, there was still plenty to do: the heap of coal on the tender had to be levelled off, in case any should fall overboard once we got moving, the engine lamps and white head code discs had to be collected from the shed and the water hose connected to fill the tender tank. Another trip was made to the shed, this time to collect a can of water treatment, which was poured in the filler hole at the back of the tender. On the Mid-Hants, the water is very hard and to stop it from scaling up the boilers we add this water treatment chemical which converts the hard scale forming salts into a soft sludge; this can later be removed via the boiler blowdown valve, which is situated at the lowest point on the firebox, just above the foundation ring.

Now that all the essential jobs had been taken care of, I took the remaining rags and paraffin to make a start with the cleaning. The nature of a steam locomotive is such that it would appear to have been especially designed to make itself dirty: in the first place, you have all the oil from around the motion, which is applied by the driver at the start of each turn of duty and then spends the rest of the shift being thrown out again by the moving parts and being distributed by the slipstream, so that finally it covers just about everything below footplate level. Then you have the clouds of dust and ash which descend from the ashpan and stick to the oily parts every time the fire is dropped, the coal dust from the tender which blows all round the cab and finally the soot from the chimney to anoint the boiler cladding. When I was a boy I used to admire all the shiny green Western engines at Paddington and turned my nose up at their dirty former London Midland & Scottish Railway (LMS) counterparts over at Euston, but now I know how much hard work it takes to clean an engine and how quickly they get filthy again, I can have some sympathy for the men at Camden shed, whilst wondering how on earth they managed to keep up the standards at Old Oak Common, almost right up to the end of steam. We only had about hour and a half before we were due off shed, so the best I could do was to brush some paraffin on the wheels, cylinders and motion work to loosen the dirt and then wiped it off, while Norman gave the boiler and tender sides a quick rub over.

After about three-quarters of an hour we had enough pressure to operate the blower and clear the smoke from the cab. Norman added a few more shovels of coal to the fire, which had now started to burn its way back up the grate from the initial heap at the front. If steam had been a bit slow coming, we could have got the long rake down from the tender and used it to pull some of the burning coals back toward the firedoor, which would soon have had the fire burning evenly all over.

John Gibbins. who was our driver for the day, had now arrived and was doing the rounds with his oil cans, so Norman suggested it was time we took a stroll back to the 'Manor' for a cup of tea. I reckoned I must have already expended more energy in that first three hours than the average office worker would in a whole day, so this seemed to be a jolly good idea.

Engine preparation is a dirty job, so after we had drunk our tea, we got changed into some clean overalls so that we could present a passable appearance to the paying public. Then it was back to the engine again via the shed, where we collected James's smiling face and gave it a quick clean over. The faces are actually large fibreglass mouldings and are pretty awkward to handle, so it was a two man job to lift it up and secure it to the smokebox door.

Back on the footplate again, things were looking a lot healthier; the fire was burning brightly all over the grate and there was 100 lb. of steam - more than enough to move the engine if we wanted to. Norman added some more coal under the firedoors and a couple more shovels further down to cover the thin places. At this stage the steam pressure could be raised very rapidly if need be, so we were pretty well ready to go. Norman got me to test the injectors and use the 'pep pipe' to give the cab floor a wash down. The pep pipe is an armoured hose connected to the delivery side off one of the injectors and produces a jet of nearly boiling water, so we had a good look round outside to ensure we didn't give anyone a face full as they walked past.

The injector is a cunning device that achieves the seemingly impossible function of using boiler pressure steam to force the feed water into the boiler against that very same pressure, in order refill it when replenishment is required. Patented by a Frenchman called Giffard (or was he a Belgian?) in 1858, the injector, in its simplest form has no moving parts and consists of a series of nozzles (or cones to those in the trade) within a housing. Steam from the boiler is expanded through the first nozzle (the steam cone) achieving supersonic speed in the process. This high velocity jet is directed into the bell-mouthed end of a second cone called the combining cone. Cold water from the tender is fed into the space between the steam and combining cones and becomes entrained in the jet. This water condenses the steam, so that at the far end of the combining cone we have a high speed jet of hot water but still at a pressure well below that of the boiler. This jet of water now jumps another gap where any excess water or uncondensed steam can escape via an overflow pipe, before entering the final cone (the delivery cone). The delivery cone is a divergent nozzle, which means that the speed of the fluid within it will be much reduced as it travels toward the end. Now a clever chap called Bernouilly once propounded a theory that the energy of the fluid passing through any closed system like this will remain constant (apart from friction and radiation losses) at all points within the system. This means that the enormous kinetic energy of the high speed water column leaving the combining cone is now converted to pressure energy as it slows down in the delivery cone, until the pressure is great enough to lift the clack valve (water inlet) and enter the boiler; and so the miracle is brought about. An injector of this type is called a live steam injector because it uses steam direct from the boiler.

Much later in the development of the steam locomotive, somebody discovered that once you had got an injector started using live steam, it could be made to continue functioning using some of the exhaust steam leaving the cylinders, that would otherwise be shot up the chimney and wasted. This meant you now had a boiler feed device that worked for nothing! Another benefit of exhaust injectors is that they heat the feed water considerably before it enters the boiler, which means a saving in coal consumption. Exhaust steam injectors are a lot more complicated than live steam ones and require additional cones, automatic changeover valves and the like. For this reason they were usually only fitted to the bigger passenger engines that ran long distances without shutting off steam. Most others, including 'James' make do with two live steam ones. To start an injector, all that is required is to turn on the water and then the steam in that order. Shutting down is done in reverse order – steam off first and then the water; if you forget and shut the water off first, a fierce blast of steam will issue from the overflow and will probably earn you a black look from the driver!

Prior to the invention of the injector, most engines used pumps driven from the axles or some part of the motion to feed the boiler. This was fine when the engine was running but what if it had to stand still for any length of time in sidings or at a signal? In such circumstances some drivers had been forced to adopt drastic measures such as oiling the rails so that wheelspin could be induced to keep the engine running on the spot, simply to work the pump - hardly a very satisfactory arrangement!

When I had finished testing and washing down, John decided it was time to make a move, so I hopped down off the engine and knocked out the wooden chocks from the driving wheels, then climbed back aboard. John gave a toot on the whistle and cracked open the regulator - nothing happened at first except that the front of the engine disappeared in a cloud of steam from the open cylinder drain cocks, but eventually enough pressure built up in the cylinders to overcome the resistance and we began to creep backwards, blowing steam all the way. When we got past the exit points, John gave another toot to advise the signalman we were clear and we waited for the road to go over (points to change) and the dummy to clear. It did so and we proceeded down to the signal box to collect the token, without which we were not permitted to go beyond station limits.

The Mid-Hants is a single line railway with three sections: Alresford to Ropley, Ropley to Medstead and Medstead to Alton. The last named has a single train staff kept in the signal box at Medstead, which must be in possession of the driver before he enters the section. If two trains in a row are going the same way, the driver of the first train is shown the staff as proof that the line is clear and is then given a ticket by the signalman which is his permit to proceed. When the signalman has been advised by the by the person in charge at Alton that the first train has arrived, the second train then follows down with the staff. This is known as 'staff and ticket' working and has one severe drawback - once the staff has gone through the section, the only permitted movement is back the other way.

The other two sections on the Mid-Hants are protected by electrically interlocked token instruments of a type invented by a brilliant signal engineer named Edward Tyer more than 100 years ago. A supply of tokens is kept in the instruments at each end of the section and when one is withdrawn from either end to permit a train movement, then both instruments become locked. Further tokens cannot be issued until the first one has been replaced at the other end of the section, thereby ensuring that there can never be more than one train in a section at a time. Several trains may follow each other through the section - up to the maximum number of tokens stored in the instrument. In the unlikely event that one instrument is about to run out of tokens, then it is possible by invoking special safety procedures by a senior signalman to unlock the instruments to remove several tokens at once and transfer them back to the instrument that needed a top-up. A foolproof system you might think and indeed, for more than 40 years from the time of their invention in 1878, there were no accidents on single line railways protected by them.

Human carelessness, however, eventually managed to defeat the system, at a sleepy little village called Abermule in Mid Wales back in 1921. A local train arrived there one day from Montgomery and the driver surrendered the token for the Montgomery to Abermule section to a member of the platform staff. This person gave it to the station master who should have replaced it in the token instrument for that section. Instead, he assumed it must have been the token for the Abermule to Newtown section that followed and gave it back to the driver. It would have been impossible to obtain a token for this section in the normal way, because it was already occupied by an express train coming down from Newtown. Even now, disaster should have been averted; if the driver of the local train had bothered to read the inscription on the token he had been given, he would have immediately spotted the mistake. However, he did not and went on to his death in the ensuing head-on collision, together with 15 passengers of the express train. This is why, 70-odd years later, Norman read 'Ropley to Alresford' out loud to the driver and then hung the token up on the back of the boiler where we could all see it.

With the token safely aboard and the starting signal cleared, we gave another toot on the whistle and puffed gently off down to hill to Alresford to pick up our train. There was not much for us to do on this leg, so Norman and I poured ourselves a cup of tea from my new tea can, which had been keeping warm on the tray above the firehole and then took it easy and admired the view.

As we ran into the cutting before Alresford, John braked the engine down to about 10 mph so we could observe the signals as they came into view around the final bend. In this case, they were clear, so we could run straight down onto our train, which was waiting in the up platform. The signalman descended from his box to collect our token as we rolled in, while the shunter stood in the six foot (the area between two running lines) by the front of the first coach and hand-signalled us forwards until we buffered up with a gentle clonk. John dropped the brake handle to destroy the vacuum and stuck a hand out from the cab to let the shunter know it was safe to go in and couple up.

Norman, possibly foolishly, seeing as he hardly knew me, had decided that I could fire the first trip, so I awaited his further instructions rather nervously. He explained that it was strictly frowned upon to allow the engine to blow off steam from the safety valves, or to make black smoke while standing in stations - especially Alresford station where we were.

The actual moment therefore to commence building up the fire ready for departure is quite critical; too soon and you will have full pressure and a full glass (maximum permitted water level) before it is time to go, in which case it is almost certain that the engine will blow off steam; once that coal has gone on the fire, you can't take it off again! If you leave it too late, then obviously you will be short of steam or water when you depart and will have a tough job to recover it.

To reduce the risk of smoke you must avoid throwing coal down to the front end of the grate, where it will quickly ignite and where there is not much air getting to it to burn it off - just one or two careless shovels down there will produce lots of the unwelcome black stuff. The only way to clear it is to open the blower some more, which will cause more air to be drawn in through the firehole to burn it off and will also shoot it higher into the air above the chimney. The snag with this ploy is that the increased draught will brighten the fire and cause the steam pressure to rise toward the red line at which the safety valves will blow off - on this engine it is set at 200 psi. Blowing off steam at the safeties is just as big a sin as making smoke and the only thing you can do now to knock the pressure back again is to add more cold water to the boiler by use of the injectors. You can keep doing this until the water level gets close to the top of the glass but then you will have to stop; any more and you run the risk of 'priming', which is where water is carried over with the steam to the cylinders when the regulator is opened. Water of course is incompressible and can cause a lot of damage - in severe cases, cylinder covers may be fractured.

From the above notes you will be able to see that the fireman has to perform quite a complicated balancing act if he is to achieve the desired full head of steam and the requisite water level at departure time. He will usually want to give himself enough space in the boiler to keep the engine quiet for a few minutes beyond the scheduled time as well, in case the train is late leaving - not unheard of even on the Mid-Hants!

About 15 minutes before departure time, Norman at last told me start building up the fire, so I picked up the shovel and got busy. After about 20 shots, all at the back end as noted above, it looked like a reasonable pile, so I gave an enquiring glance in Norman's direction but he just motioned me to keep going. Another 15 shots and another enquiry but the answer was still the same. Eventually, when my heap of coal was level with the bottom of the firehole, Norman called a halt, so I could straighten my back and take a breather for a minute or two.

With around five minutes to go, I was instructed to extend this heap forwards by throwing a few shovels down the sides, which began to form the desired wedge-shaped fire - and also produced some black smoke at the chimney, which I swiftly dissipated by cracking open the blower a bit more. We also opened the damper a notch, which allowed air to enter the fire from beneath the grate, thereby speeding the steam raising process. With the pressure now rising toward the red line, I put on the injector and used the pep pipe to wash down the footplate and spray over the coal, as we would be travelling tender first on this trip and didn't want the slipstream to blow coal dust back over us.

The signalman now strolled over with the token, which we hung in its appointed place, the starting signal at the end of the platform was cleared, so all we needed was the tip from the guard. Norman had timed our preparation to perfection, the pressure gauge was nearly on the mark and we had three-quarters of a glass of water. John wound the engine into full reverse gear and leaned out of the cab to watch for the guard's signal. Soon we heard a whistle from the platform and the guard waved his green flag. 'Right away' yelled John, then he gave a pull on the whistle cord, opened the regulator and we began to move, the firedoors slapping in their runners with each heavy exhaust beat, as we slogged away under the road bridge and up the 1 in 80 through the cutting toward Ropley.

Instructions now came thick and fast in my direction: 'Close the doors', 'Not too much', 'Watch the smoke', 'Knock that injector off', 'Get ready to fire again', etc. As we had not yet put any coal down the front end of the grate, this is where the first round had to go. 'Three down each side and two down the middle' was Norman's recipe and I did my best to comply while he opened and shut the firedoors between shots for me. 'Give it some more welly' was his immediate cry, closely followed by 'Swing the shovel don't poke it'. I gave a mighty swing in order to provide the desired amount of 'welly' but the shovel caught the bottom of the firehole, the shock nearly paralysed my arm and my coal was spread nicely over the floor. Norman grinned and remarked 'If that last one had only gone through the hole it would have been perfect!'

Despite my ineptitude, at least some of my shovel shots must have been hitting their mark because there was a bit of smoke at the chimney, which was a good sign. Although we have to avoid making smoke in stations, if you fire a round of coal when the engine is out on the road working and don't get any smoke when you shut the firedoors, it means that you've chucked it in the wrong place. Fresh coal should always be added to the brightest part of the fire for immediate combustion to take place, and smoke is the sign that this has occurred.

After a few seconds the smoke had cleared again, so my mentor called for another round in the prescribed manner, which I duly swung in. This time when we closed the doors, there was quite a bit of smoke and the steam pressure, which had sagged to 175 psi in the first half mile had started to climb again, so I was obviously winning. Norman motioned for me to put on the injector again now that the water level had started to drop. I waited again for the smoke to clear and fired one more round, which Norman deemed would be sufficient to see us to Ropley.

This is the shortest of the three sections on the railway, so we didn't want to arrive in the station with a box of unburned fuel and then have the safeties blowing off, which would let all the gawpers at the shed know we had overdone it. If you have timed everything right, all the fuel will be well burned through by the time the driver shuts off steam for the station, so by standing by to put on the injectors if need be, the engine can be kept quiet when the regulator is closed. As we approached the shutting-off point the blower was opened wide to avoid any possibility of a blow back through the firedoors; the tremendous fire at this stage is so hungry for oxygen, that if there is insufficient blast to draw air in through the firehole, the only other way the flames can get it is to shoot back out into the cab and fry the crew in the process!

As the home signal came into sight, John shut off steam and I opened the firedoors and put on the second injector. The fire was still blinding white at this point but now that the volatile content had been burned off, what was left was more akin to coke than coal and soon died down without the draught from the chimney on it.

As we rolled to a stand opposite the signal box, the signalman took our token from us and retreated back into his cabin with it. The fire appeared to be under control, so I could shut off the injectors and take a look. I was amazed at how much fuel we had burnt; my big heap under the door had dropped down nearly a foot and Norman told me to get busy and fill it up again, as we would be on our way as soon as the down train arrived from Medstead. After a couple of minutes we heard the melodious note of a chime whistle and No. 73096, our BR Standard class '5' 4-6-0 slid into view from beneath the road bridge and rumbled on into the down platform.

We could hear the block bells ringing as the bobby (signalman) sent the message 'train out of section' to Medstead and replaced the token from No. 73096 back in Mr Tyer's Victorian fruit machine to clear the block section. Now that he had done this, a few more dings to ask Medstead if the line was clear to accept us into the section and he could withdraw our token and pull off the starting signal for us. He inserted the token into a leather pouch with a large grab ring on it and handed it up to us on the footplate. After checking it was correct, we turned our attention to the guard on the platform, who immediately gave us the 'right away', so we were off again. John took the engine carefully over the points from the up platform loop onto the running line and once the last coach had cleared the points he opened up on 50 per cent cut-off and first valve of the regulator to accelerate the train away. After the road bridge, the gradient stiffens to about 1 in 60 and John now gave the engine full regulator and 40 per cent cut-off, at which setting our gallant steed was really blasting away up the hill.

I now started firing again using Norman's usual formula of 'three down the sides and two down the middle' at fairly frequent intervals. This time however, things did not seem to be going so well; the steam pressure dropped about 15 psi after the initial start and showed no signs of recovery. After about a mile, the injector had to go on to maintain the water level in the boiler and this immediately sent the clock even further the wrong way. There was very little smoke at the chimney, which indicated that something was wrong with the fire but as yet I didn't know what. John eased the engine back a little to conserve steam - he looked exasperated but said nothing. Eventually we came round the last bend and onto the long straight leading up to Medstead. That last mile seemed to take an interminable time and the boiler pressure continued to decline. I went to put some more coal on but Norman said not to bother, because we would be shutting off before it would have time to do any good. Finally, we crawled into the platform with about 140 pounds of steam and barely a couple of inches of water in the glass.

When we had stopped, Norman had a good look in the box to see what had gone wrong - it appeared that some of my long shots had dropped short and formed a bit of a ridge halfway down the grate, thus preventing all subsequent coal from reaching the front. Norman got down the pricker (a long fire iron with the end bent

No. 73096 beside Ropley signal box. *Author*

'Thomas' with two young admirers at Ropley in 2007. *Author/© 2008 Gullane (Thomas) Ltd*

over at a right angle) from the tender and levelled the fire over, which immediately produced plenty of smoke and proved that there had been more than enough fuel in the box if it had only been thrown in the right places. Naturally I was feeling a bit despondent, but Norman said he has seen worse - and at least he hadn't snatched the shovel out of my hand to put things right, for which I was grateful.

We were working a shuttle service from Ropley to Medstead, so now we had to uncouple and run round the train before going back down the hill again. During 'Thomas' week it was the normal arrangement to have 'James' doing this turn and 'Thomas' running Alresford to Ropley shuttles, while the bigger engines operated the two service trains over the full length of the line. These short shuttle services allowed more families a chance to ride behind 'Thomas' and 'James', which were the main attractions for the younger children. In any event, 'Thomas', with his small wheels and limited water capacity would be hard put to maintain the schedule if he had to work over the entire line.

On our way back down to Ropley, Norman had me practising my shovel shots by firing one small lump of coal at a time to various parts of the firebox. This was a clever ploy and enabled me to get in plenty of shovel swinging without actually putting much on the fire. Practice is of course hard to come by otherwise, as most volunteers will only have around 15 rostered firing turns a year and unless they are fortunate enough to be able to take a few mid-week turns as well, the learning curve has to be pretty steep.

We had another five of these shuttles to work today and Norman and I took each one in turn. I am pleased to report that my second and third attempts were blessed with better results than the first one - in fact for my last go, I overdid the firing on the way up and the engine blew off steam nearly all the way back down to Ropley, which earned me another pained expression from John!

After the final run, we put our coaches to bed in the headshunt at Alresford, before running light engine back to the shed. Norman used the pricker again to level over the fire and got me to bring down some small coal and dust to fire on the way back. He pointed out to me that even without the coaches, we were still taking more than one hundred tons up hill, so even this would require a fair bit of steam. By using just small coal, it would all burn away before our arrival, which would avoid taking the engine on shed with too much fire in the box.

Back at Ropley we ran into the down platform and surrendered the token to the signalman for the last time as we passed his box. Then we continued up the pit road for some way and blew the boiler down. For this to be worthwhile, the pressure should be somewhere near the maximum, together with a full glass of water. John got down off the engine and after ensuring there was nobody anywhere near the discharge pipe, opened the blowdown valve. The noise of the escaping steam was deafening and everything disappeared in a white cloud. It was pointless trying to shout at John when the level had dropped to the required half a glass, so we blew the whistle instead to let him know. When he had shut the valve, silence mercifully reigned once more and our surroundings returned to view as the steam dissipated.

It is interesting to observe that although the blowdown valve is situated in the water space at the lowest point of the boiler, it is steam and not water that blasts out when it is opened. This is because the boiling point of water increases with the pressure, so that at 200 psi the temperature in James's boiler is 194 degrees Celsius and not 100, as it would be in a domestic kettle. As soon as the blowdown valve is opened, the emerging water instantly flashes off into vast quantities of steam (260 cubic feet for each gallon of water released), which is why steam boiler explosions are so devastating. The converse is also true - at pressures below normal atmospheric, the boiling point decreases, which is why you will never get a decent cup of tea at the top of Mount Everest - not a lot of people know that!

It was now 6 pm and having been working hard for 12 hours, I was feeling pretty tired but there was still more to be done before we were finished. First of all, we ran forward to the coal stage where John drove our somewhat dilapidated digger and refilled the tender, while I stood on top to keep the growing heap levelled off between loads and to prevent any lumps from falling over the sides. Then we continued down the pit road as far as we could, to allow the next engine to take coal.

At our final resting place, John wound the engine into mid-gear and opened the cylinder cocks, the handbrake was screwed on and the chocks were placed under the wheels. Now came another unpleasant chore: remove James's face, open the smokebox door and shovel out all the char that had accumulated during the day. Norman did the shovelling out, while I ran back and forth with the wheelbarrow to the ash dump; we took out three barrow loads in total. Having closed the door again I swept the spilt ash off the front framing and buffers - if this was not done carefully, it could blow back in the driver's eyes when the engine next went out.

Next on the list was to collect enough wood for the following crew to light the fire and stack it in a corner of the cab. Meanwhile, John had been busy refilling the boiler from the injector and giving the cab floor a good hose down with the pep pipe to lay the dust from the coaling operation. The last job of all was to close all the steam valves in the cab and shut off the water gauges, before we could finally kiss the engine good night and take our weary bodies off home.

Norman had proved to be a very good instructor and had the patience to allow me to make a few mistakes, so that I could find out for myself what I was doing wrong - a much quicker way to learn than if he had continually interfered and taken the shovel from me to put things right himself.

So ended my first turn on the footplate. I have described all the basic procedures in some detail, in an attempt to show that there is rather more to being a locomotive fireman than just throwing coal on a fire.

When I got home, the number one priority was to grab a cold beer from the fridge, which disappeared pretty rapidly and was followed by another. Then a nice long shower – how did all that coal dust fetch up in my hair? With a clean body and some clean clothes I began to feel civilised again, despite a few aches and pains from my exertions. Not being accustomed to the job, I had found it pretty hard going but immensely enjoyable. Although I had experienced a few previous footplate trips, this was the first time anyone offered me the chance to take the shovel and have a go, so if you ever get to read this Norman, thanks very much mate.

Chapter Four

Experience Gained and Some Weight Lost

My next turn came up in December, when the railway was running 'Santa Specials'. These services are again aimed at the younger generation and involve Father Christmas travelling on the train, together with mince pies and similar seasonal treats being proffered to the passengers.

The engine on this occasion was No. 73096, a BR Standard class '5' 4-6-0, very similar to the famous 'Black Fives' of the LMS. Before they were constructed, the design team actually went to the trouble of constructing a wooden mock-up of the cab layout, which would be common to all the Standard classes and inviting enginemen of the various Regions to come along and say what they thought of it. The result was a pleasant roomy cab, with all the driver's controls arranged on his side, where they could be operated from the sitting position. Similarly, the injector and damper controls were conveniently placed on the fireman's side. The essential blower valve was fitted to the brake valve plinth, where either man could reach it quickly. Naturally, the new design did not appeal to everyone - the Great Western fraternity in particular, were amongst the most critical; for a start off, the new engines were left-hand drive, whereas the GWR engines were all right-handed and their signals had been installed to be most visible from that side. The LMS men were also a bit sniffy - they already regarded their 'Black Fives' as the best mixed traffic engine in the country and could see no reason to alter it in any way. I think however, that an unbiased observer would stand back and say that the 'Standard 5' was the better engine, although not by very much. The 'bacon slicer' reverse wheel of the new engines was certainly easier to operate than the conventional type, which faced the driver like a car steering wheel, while the longer valve travel and slightly bigger wheels with roller bearing axles made them a little more free running.

When I first climbed aboard and had a look in the firebox, I could see that it was over a foot longer than on the 'N' class, which made me feel a bit apprehensive - I had enough difficulty getting the coal down to the front of that box and so this one could only be worse. The reader may wonder what is the problem with throwing coal a mere 9½ feet? I can remember one time when I had a load of pea shingle delivered to my home and needed to spread it around part of my back yard - it was quite easy to throw it twice that far in one swing. However, an examination of the trajectory would show that the gravel was going in a nice curve upwards before coming down again. This method would be useless on an engine, because the coal would be hitting the baffle plate or the brick arch on the way. So you need to keep the shovel handle high and propel the coal down parallel to the slope of the firebed - and if you don't do it fast enough, it will drop short. The swing then, needs to be fast and flat, at the required downward angle and last but not least, has to go through the firehole - this itself takes a bit of practice, as there is only a couple of inches clearance on either side of the shovel as it goes in. Naturally, when you miss (and who hasn't), the shock on your hands and arms is quite painful and may further

No. 73096 stands beside Ropley signal box and waits for the token in 2005. *Author*

The author's favourite engine - BR Standard class '5' No. 73096 runs into Ropley with a down train. *R. Forster*

inhibit your action. Just to make it even more difficult, this engine was left-hand drive, which meant, strictly speaking, that the fireman should stand on the right and fire left-handed – and I couldn't even do it properly right-handed yet!

On this occasion I managed to turn up before the fireman (Norman again), and had made a start on cleaning the fire by the time he arrived. He said he had come off his motorbike and hurt his arm and would probably only fire the first trip just to give me an idea, after which she would be mine for the rest of the day - or at least until I screwed up sufficiently badly for him to have to take over again!

We prepared the engine in a leisurely fashion as there was still 40 lb. of steam on the clock from the previous day. I should explain here that that it is standard practice on the Mind-Hants, that an engine will be lit up and steam raised on the day before it goes into traffic; the fire then being allowed to go out again overnight. This avoids the necessity of finding someone willing to spend all night in the lonely and thankless task of fire lighting and steam raising. How much steam and water is left in the boiler when the fireman turns up around 6 am varies considerably. The ideal would probably be about a quarter glass of water and at least 20 lb. of steam. If there is a full glass when you start, there will be no room left in the boiler to add more and you may have difficulty keeping the engine quiet when you arrive down at Alresford on the first trip. In such circumstances, the fireman may elect to let some out via the blowdown valve before lighting up. If on the other hand, the glass is empty in the morning - invariably a sign of leakage somewhere, then the boiler will have to be topped up with a firehose connected to the injector overflow pipe. As water expands when heated, an inch showing in the gauge is enough to start with; this will rise to nearly half a glass by the time steam is raised.

By the time our driver Chris Churm had joined us, we had got around 100 lb. of steam and Norman had done most of the oiling. On this engine, lubrication is a pretty easy job, as all the oiling points can be reached comfortably from the outside. Leaving Chris to carry on, we retired to the 'Manor' to have a cup of tea and get changed. By now I had a proper set of engineman's overalls to wear - these are dark blue when new and gradually fade down to a very pale grey/blue with repeated washes, so my inexperience was plain for all to see.

Back aboard No. 73096, we had a final clean round and then trundled off down to Alresford to pick up our train. On arrival, I nipped into the buffet to get us some more tea - this being as important for the crews as water is for the engine. As Norman was firing this trip, I could stand back and drink mine in peace, while he plied the shovel and built the fire up, which on this occasion seemed to me to be a particularly big one. I had a closer look and could see it was right up to the firehole ring and built forward level for a couple of feet more, before sloping steeply down to the front - enough to have got us to Guildford I would have thought, never mind Alton. I remarked on how much coal there was in the box to Norman but he said to just wait and see.

When we got the right away, Chris blew the whistle and got the train moving; it was immediately apparent that he was not the same sort of driver as I had last time and he fairly blasted the engine out of the station. By the time we passed under Sun Lane bridge, which is not much more than 100 yards from the end of the platform, the regulator was full open with the reverser on 50 per cent cut-off; the noise from the chimney was awesome and I half expected it to fly off. Another 100 yards and the cut-off was brought back to 40 per cent, but that's where it stayed; Norman's carefully built fire was disappearing rapidly and he started firing again. Despite the hammering, No. 73096 seemed to lap it up and the pressure gauge began to climb, so Norman banged on the exhaust injector to stop the engine blowing off and to maintain the water level. We continued like this for the next couple of miles with Norman firing several of his favourite pattern of 'three down the sides and two down the middle', to keep the recommended degree of brown smoke at the chimney. When Ropley distant came into sight, the damper was closed and the blower opened, before steam was finally shut off. Then, the fire doors were opened wide, the second injector went on to keep the engine quiet and we rolled into the platform looking as innocent as could be.

Norman used the brief stop in Ropley to bang another two dozen or so big shovels on, to rebuild the back end of the fire before we departed. This second leg up to Medstead, which is about a mile longer than the first, followed much the same pattern, with the engine getting a good thrashing and appearing to thrive on it.

When we stopped in the platform, I could have a closer look at the fire - that huge heap at the back had all but disappeared and the rest of the grate looked pretty thin - Norman saw my raised eyebrows but just sat back on his seat with a 'told you so' sort of expression on his face.

We had five of these Alresford-Medstead specials to work, so we ran round the train and were soon on our way back down the hill again. Norman handed me the shovel and told me to get in some more practice with my long shots by filling the thinner places on the fire using the patent 'one lump at a time' technique - I was very relieved that neither he nor Chris were expecting me to do it left-handed.

After we had got back to Alresford and run round the train again, there was only about 20 minutes left before departure, so I got busy immediately and built up another whacking great fire - this took at least 50 shots at the back end just for starters! Norman seemed happy with this and then got me to throw another dozen down each side and finally three or four more rolled down the slope in the middle, to complete the job. We had a fair bit of blower to lift the smoke and the pressure rose towards the red line which is 225 psi on this engine, so on went the injector to avoid blowing off. By the time we got the right away, we had nearly a full glass of water and 220 psi, so I had given myself a good start.

We thundered under the bridge and into the cutting and it was obvious that Chris was taking no prisoners on this trip either - rooky fireman or not. I waited until he notched up to the usual 40 per cent cut-off and then banged half a dozen shots as far down the front as I could, with Norman opening and closing the firedoors for me between throws. A quick glance at the chimney showed rather more smoke than it should, so we cracked open the doors a couple of inches to give it a bit more air. It soon cleared, which meant it was time for another round. I found that my worries about the long firebox were unfounded, the heavy blast was sucking so much air through the firehole that it whipped the coal off the shovel and where it had to go without any great effort, and in any case, I also noted that the front of the box didn't seem to need very much added after the initial round had gone down there.

One other thing I soon discovered about this engine was how hot the tray above the firehole became; when making long shots with the arm extended, it was very easy to touch this with the forearm just above the wrist and receive a minor burn, which left a very faint pink scar when it healed. I have collected quite a few of these scars over the years from No. 73096 and when I eventually learned to fire left-handed, I got a matching set on the other arm as well!

I was not finding it quite so easy as Norman on this trip but still managed to keep the pressure up around the 200 psi mark against the injector, which was more than enough for our five-coach train, even on the 1 in 60. The next couple of runs were rather better and Norman said I seemed to be getting the hang of it, which cheered me up considerably. Norman elected to fire the last trip after all, so I could sit down for a change and have a final swill of tea from the can, which of course was well stewed by now - funny how I couldn't stand tea as a boy.

After we had shunted our coaches at the end of the day, it was back to Ropley to dispose of the engine and it was my turn to empty the smokebox. I loosened the central bolt on the smokebox door (the outer of the two handles), which allowed the other one (the dart) to be rotated through 90 degrees and then swung open the door. I was unprepared for the amount of char in there and a minor avalanche cascaded out onto the front framing and over my feet - some found its way into my boots and for the next few seconds I was jumping about like a demented monkey until the heat went off. Altogether we shovelled out six barrow loads, which Norman reckoned was a pretty good indication of how hard the engine had been worked.

Apart from a trip on the 'S15' class 4-6-0 on which I didn't get a chance to fire, my next outing was not until the Easter 'Thomas' event. I had put my name down two days in a row and thought that I should strike lucky at least once.

When I turned up for the first one and looked for the engine number on the board, I saw it was No. 5080, which made me do a double take - if memory served, this must be another Great Western 'Castle'- and so it proved. This one wasn't actually named after a castle but was called *Defiant*, indicating that it had been built during the war when several of the class were named after RAF aircraft. I hoped it would be a rather better performer today that its namesake, which was a singularly useless aeroplane. Even back in World War I, it was the generally accepted view that fighter aircraft should get behind the enemy to shoot them down, so it is amazing that someone should have designed this one with its main armament being a four gun turret that only fired backwards and sideways!

My mates on the day were driver Mick Austen and fireman Richard Faithful - the latter being at least 20 years my junior but very good at his job nonetheless. We climbed up on the footplate to take stock of our unfamiliar machine. Compared to the Standard class '5', with its nice cosy cab, the footplate seemed to be very exposed, having a much lower tender front and more open cab sides. The Great Western obviously believed their men were tough enough to do without much in the way of creature comforts - there were not even any doors between engine and tender to stop you falling out!

We noted that there was only one gauge glass, although a set of three test cocks were also provided in case the glass failed. As I have explained earlier, when water under pressure is let out of a boiler, it flashes off instantly into steam, so I have always been a bit dubious of the value of test cocks.

Very prominent on the floor next to the firehole, were the four levers which operated the dampers. Because this engine has such a long firebox, the ashpan is in two sections spanning the trailing axle, with a damper at the front and rear of each. They were not labelled, so I got down below in the pit and observed whilst Richard operated them in turn, so we could establish which one was which.

The firehole doors are of the double sliding variety, the same as on No. 73096 and have a similar flap arrangement, hinged at the bottom. When the flap is raised, it leaves a small gap above it to admit top air when required. The flap on No. 73096 however has a bigger gap and small coal can be fired over it, which is quite a useful feature. The gap on this one is too small for firing purposes and it has to be dropped for each shovel shot - there is a chain connecting the top of the flap to the main firedoor handle to facilitate this.

We found an absolute mountain of coal on the tender, which needed quite a bit of levelling off to make it safe. I didn't think we would use anything like this much coal on four round trips, but as the day unfolded it showed just how wrong you could be.

Lighting up and preparation followed exactly the same pattern as usual, except that we had rather more firebox to fill up than on No. 73096. I should mention here that all narrow firebox engines, from small shunters up to large express types such as this, where the boiler has to sit between the frames, will have pretty much the same width of firebox - the frame separation and hence the firebox width, being fixed by the gauge of the track. This means that to obtain a bigger grate area, the only thing you can do is to increase the length - on this engine it is about 10 feet long, giving 30 square feet of grate area. Only a very few engines, including the Great Western 'King' class and the Southern 'Lord Nelsons' had longer fireboxes than this. As the power of an engine is to a large extent determined by its ability to burn coal (gospel according to Bulleid) and to burn more coal means having ever bigger grate areas, eventually it becomes necessary to adopt the wide firebox design, where the firebox spans the frames. All the big four companies except the Great Western, eventually adopted wide firebox 'Pacific' types, with up to fifty square feet of grate for their main line express engines. The Great Western, having built the first British Pacific in 1908 (called *The Great Bear*), decided they didn't really need engines that big and stayed with 4-6-0s right up to the end of steam.

Mick, meanwhile, was crawling around under the engine, complaining about all the oiling points he had to find - as this was a four-cylinder engine with two sets of Walschaerts valve gear and motion between the frames, there were a great many. No doubt there is an optimum position of the wheels for getting at all of these but as we were hemmed in by another engine and had no steam to move anyway, Mick had to do it as it stood.

Essentially, a 'Castle' is an enlarged 'Star' class engine - Churchward's masterpiece of 1906. The first of these was built as an Atlantic (4-4-2) and called *North Star*. The remainder were redesigned as 4-6-0s, thereby setting the pattern for all further Great Western express engines. *Defiant* then, is basically an Edwardian engine, constructed with elegance rather than ease of maintenance in mind, hence the inside valve gear with derived motion for the outside cylinders. When Sir William Stanier designed his famous 'Coronation' Pacifics 30 years later, which have exactly the same four-cylinder arrangement, he did things the other way round, putting the valve gear outside with derived motion for the inside cylinders, which of course made things a lot easier to get at.

Whatever shortcomings the engine may have had, and by now we had also found that there were leaking tubes in the firebox and a loose deflector plate, I was still thrilled to bits to be on it. Having always been a fan of the Great Western, I could remember the many occasions when I had stood at the end of one of the platforms at Paddington station, watching the morning procession of expresses depart, mostly with gleaming 'Kings' and 'Castles' at their head and being green with envy of the crews. I never imagined that one day I would get the chance to fire one myself, but here we were.

As this was 'Thomas' week again, *Defiant* was pretending to be 'Henry the Green Engine' and even had some nice 'Henry' nameplates made up to fit in place of the real ones. With the engine well cleaned up and his face wiped, we looked quite convincing as we rumbled off shed and down to pick up our train, which was six coaches for a change instead of the usual five.

GWR 'Castle' class 4-6-0 No. 5080 *Defiant* pretending to be 'Henry the Green Engine' stands at Ropley in 1995; driver Andrew Netherwood beside.

Author/© 2008 Gullane (Thomas) Ltd

Richard elected to fire the first and third trips and generously offered me the other two, which gave me a chance to see how he did it. One thing about being a third man and working with different crews, is that you find no two firemen do things exactly the same way and what suited your previous mate may well not be viewed favourably by the next. It was good therefore that I could see Richard perform first and also find out what sort of a driver we had.

The basic formula turned out to be exactly the same as on the other engines I had seen, with the fire built right up to the doors at the back and tapering down to about one lump thick at the front. The firebox was very deep at the back end and took a lot of filling, while I could see that it would take a mighty swing to get it all the way down the front. One thing we soon discovered was that with the dampers closed and the fire doors open, the fire died down very quickly and we had no difficulty at any time in keeping the engine quiet - in fact it seemed to need a fair bit of blower to stop the pressure going down even, when standing in stations.

Mick also turned out to be quite a hard hitter and when we got the 'right away' we accelerated very rapidly out of the station with not a hint of wheelslip and with that wonderful Great Western exhaust beat bouncing back at us from the sides of the cutting. Richard tended to fire just five or six shots at a time at frequent intervals and soon had the pressure up on the red line, which is mostly where it stayed with him firing - you would have thought he did this every day for a living, instead of which it was his first go on a 'Castle' - I was most impressed.

We were running chimney first out of Alresford today and Richard reminded me that we would need at least three-quarters of a glass of water at Medstead before we could go over the summit. The gradient changes very abruptly here from 1 in 200 up, to 1 in 60 down and as the engine passes this point, the water runs forward in the boiler and the level in the gauge will drop around six inches.

This is actually the easier way to work the engine, because if the water level is a bit low at Medstead, you have the station stop to put things right before going over the top. Coming up from Alton chimney first, however, there is no such opportunity for recovery and the water level must be kept right up to the top of the glass all the way up the climb. Apart from the change in gradient, the water level also drops when the regulator is closed and most drivers will do this briefly just before the top, so that they can see the true level. The final part of the equation is the need to stop in the station, which is just over the summit - the braking has to be done as gently as possible because this too will send all water down the front of the boiler - the level will usually disappear completely for a few seconds as the train comes to the final stop and the glass will be watched anxiously for it to reappear.

The danger of allowing the water level to get too low, is of course that the firebox crown may be uncovered and the fusible plug melt - this is called 'dropping the plug' and is a heinous crime for any engine crew to commit. The plugs are actually bronze bushes with a lead-filled centre and screw into the firebox crown. There are between one and four fitted to a boiler depending on how big it is. All the time the plugs are covered by water the lead will remain intact, but if they are uncovered, the lead will melt within seconds and the resulting inrush of steam into the firebox will alert the crew to the low water level, so they can hastily put on the injectors and then throw the fire out. If the firebox crown remains uncovered, the intense heat will cause it to soften and collapse under the pressure and a catastrophic explosion may result.

No such disasters befell us, however, and the trip passed without incident, although Richard said we were using an awful lot of coal and water. Mick reckoned that either the valve or piston rings were leaking past to exhaust, which would help account for this, but otherwise he seemed perfectly at home with his new charge.

When it was my turn to have a go, Richard suggested I started making up the fire before we actually got to Alresford; such was the appetite for coal that he reckoned that it would be cutting it a bit fine to leave it all to do in the station. It seemed to be a lot harder work than on our other engines because the shovelling plate of the tender was level with the cab floor, instead of being set at the same height as the firehole. This meant that every shovel of coal had to be lifted up about a foot before swinging it into the box. Over the course of a day, this amounted to an awful lot of extra foot pounds of energy that had to be expended.

The deflector plate was very distorted and loose in the firehole and every time the shovel gave it the slightest knock, it became partially dislodged and had to be lifted and bashed back into place with the blade of the shovel. This aside, the engine was very free steaming and quite easy to fire - even I managed to hit the red line occasionally, but we were certainly shifting the coal at an alarming rate. The wretched tender had such a shallow slope that it would not trim down on its own and after this trip, every time we stopped at either end of the line, whichever man was not firing was back in the tender shovelling it forward.

The rest of the day passed in similar fashion, with the locomotive going great guns, Mick grinning like a Cheshire cat and Richard and I working like the proverbial coloured gentlemen to keep the beast fed and watered. At one time I began to wonder if the coal supply would last out but Mick reckoned we would make it, which we eventually did, with just a few hundredweights left. Finally the day came to an end and we took the engine over the pit and disposed of it. Mick drove the digger and reloaded us with coal, stacking it up higher than the cab roof, while Richard and I emptied the smokebox. The char in there was nearly up to the dart; I didn't actually count the number of barrows we shifted but it was definitely into double figures.

By this time I was feeling well and truly shattered and had definitely had enough of steam engines to last me quite a while; maybe 48 was too old to start this lark after all. Hold on a minute though, didn't I put myself down for tomorrow as well? I checked the board in the 'Manor' and sure enough, there was my name written down. Guess what - the engine number was 5080 again!

When the alarm sounded at 4.30 am the following morning, the temptation to turn over and go back to sleep was almost irresistible. Bed at this hour is at its most inviting and my wife was muttering something about needing my brains tested but I eventually managed to drag myself up. My back was so stiff that I could hardly stand up straight and my arms felt like they had been through a mangle -

could this be the end of my love affair with steam? However, by the time I had drunk a cup of coffee, swallowed some toast and got out into the fresh air, I began to feel a little better. I have never been very keen on the actual getting up bit of an early start, but having done so, always reckoned it was the best time of the day.

The Hog's Back was still shrouded in mist as I drove over it and further down beyond Farnham, the verges were full of rabbits. The spring foliage on the many trees beside the A31 looked wonderfully lush and green and by the time I turned into the yard at Ropley, I was feeling mentally refreshed at least and ready for another dose of unpaid hard labour.

My latest driver was Andrew Netherwood, the head boilermaker of the MHR, with fireman Doug Mills. The latter turned out to be as good a mate to me as Richard had been the day before and let me do half the firing - which was a bit of mixed blessing, given the state of my back and arms. Andrew commented on the huge pile of coal on the tender and looked a little sceptical when I told him we had burnt a similar amount the day before.

Our trips followed much the same pattern as on the previous day, with no shortage of steam and plenty of shovelling to do. On one occasion I seemed to be struggling a bit, so Doug had a good squint at the fire. He could see that some of my long shots had dropped short, probably due to a lack of 'welly' from my tired arms. This had formed a bit of a hump three-quarters of the way down the box, so it was just a matter of getting out the long rake and pushing the coal forward, which soon had the pressure gauge going the right way again.

Just for an experiment, we had a try at the Great Western firing technique, which was to leave the doors open and the flap up, dropping it with the chain for each shot and then restoring it with the shovel blade afterwards. Neither of us reckoned very much of this palaver and we soon reverted to our normal method, which was to open the doors, throw in half a dozen rapid fire shots and then close them again. To be fair, the Great Western used a shovel which was twice the size of anyone else's, so maybe that made it worthwhile doing.

The only other real incident of the day was when I managed to hit the already loose deflector plate rather harder than usual and it fell into the fire. We were about half a mile out of Alton and really blasting up the hill when this happened and Andrew decided we would have to stop to fish it out. Of course, we had a great box full of fire, so the engine was blowing its head off at the safety valves while we struggled with the fire-irons and shovel to extract it. When we finally got it out, it was glowing bright red and well and truly battered out of shape, so we just dropped it in a corner of the cab and carried on without it. Andrew re-started the train up the 1 in 100 gradient without slipping and we accelerated rapidly away.

The ability of this high stepping engine to get hold of a train on a gradient is one of its most surprising features and is just as impressive now as it must have been in 1925, when one of them was sent over to the LNER at Kings Cross on an unofficial exchange trial and soundly thrashed the resident and much larger Pacifics. Some commentators noted that the 'Castle' had got to Finsbury Park in the time it took the Pacific and its train to clear Gasworks tunnel! Sir Nigel Gresley, the locomotive superintendent of the LNER, was not the sort of man who was afraid to admit a mistake and immediately set about redesigning his

Pacifics with a longer travel valve gear and higher pressure boilers in Great Western fashion. When these modified engines appeared in 1927, they were amongst the best in the country and with further development became the 'A4s' of record breaking fame.

This time when we disposed of the engine at the end of the day, I counted the barrows of char we removed from the smokebox. The grand total was 13, which remains the most I have ever seen taken from any engine on the Mid-Hants - and was at least twice as much as there was coal left in the tender!

Two questions were nagging at me as I staggered back to the 'Manor' for a wash up. Firstly, back in their heyday, a 'Castle' with that much coal would have been expected to take a 12-coach train from Paddington to Exeter or occasionally to Plymouth (which is 225 miles), with some to spare, so how come we had used it up with six coaches and 80 miles? Apart from the incident with the deflector plate, we hadn't wasted any by letting the engine blow off steam, so where did it all go? Secondly, how did those firemen in the steam era stand doing this sort of thing every day on their own, when it had nearly killed me in just two days, even though I had only done half the work!

On the way off shed, I spotted Bob Deeth (our locomotive boss) and put those questions to him - he grinned a bit when he saw the state I was in, but explained that stopping passenger trains were often harder work than the expresses, especially on a line like ours, where four round trips means 40 miles of hills to climb and 12 restarts against the gradient. An express train, once it was up to speed, had plenty of momentum and could run long distances with very little steam on a favourable road. It also has to be said that *Defiant* was not in very good nick and a 'Castle' on top form would have been a lot more economical. As for the fireman, they would not be expected to light up and dispose of their own engines as well as running the trains.

Despite giving me two of the hardest days' work in my life, I remain an unrepentant admirer of the Great Western in general and 'Castles' in particular. I am not saying that there aren't any better or more powerful engines around, but for me at any rate, they are the most beautiful. One glimpse of that classic outline, set off by the polished brass and the copper-capped chimney will always be enough to make my heart skip a beat and set me to wondering whether there isn't something more to a steam engine than just the inanimate metal from which it is made.

Many people have commented that the steam locomotive is more like a living creature than any other man-made object. I have sometimes wondered where this idea came from. Perhaps it was from the Ancient Greeks, who believed that life sprang from the four elemental forces: earth, air, fire and water, which are all there in a steam locomotive. The fire and the water are obvious, coal is of the earth, and when it is working hard, the engine may be so hungry for air that it can suck the coal off the shovel, so there you have it.

Another couple of weeks went past before my next turn came up, which was on our American 'S160' class 2-8-0, named *Franklin D. Roosevelt* – usually somewhat cheekily known as 'Frank the Yank'. Built by Baldwin in 1944, this engine worked in Italy and Greece, before being shipped back to England in 1984 and restored to running order. A big, powerful machine and the first I had

American heavy freight engine: Baldwin 'S160' class 2-8-0 No. 3278 *Franklin D. Roosevelt* at Ropley. *Tony Wood*

Baldwin 'S160' class 2-8-0 No. 3278 stands at Alreford in 1995 - this engine is no longer on the Mid Hants Railway. *Author*

fired with a wide firebox. Like the 'Castle', this engine was also right-hand drive, so I was again excused the difficulties of trying to learn left-handed firing.

As a boy, I used to detest American engines, where beauty of line always took second place to the accessibility of the works, but I have mellowed a bit over the years and have to admit that they have a certain presence. It is a case of 'horses for courses' and a 'Castle' would look just as much out of place on the New York Central as the big 'Yank' does on this bit of the old London & South Western.

I was paired up with Norman again firing and driver Roger Thornton; it was not a particularly nice morning, with a cold breeze blowing and a hint of drizzle in the air, so I was glad when Norman got the fire alight and I could join him in the cab for a warm up. Clambering up onto the high footplate, the first impression was of a spacious but cosy cab, well protected from the elements. The cab roof extended well back and enclosed the front of the enormous tender, so it should keep the draft off our backs when working tender first. The main difference in the controls were the injectors, which were operated by single pull-out handles on either side of the cab, instead of the more usual hand wheels. There was also a turbine driven electric generator which provided lights in the cab and elsewhere around the engine - quite a luxury. The regulator was a horizontal pull-out lever with a pawl and ratchet arrangement to lock it in the desired position. It was actually very insensitive and heartily disliked by all the drivers I have met - indeed, I think I have seen this engine slip more times on starting than any other type. The grate was wide but quite shallow because the ashpan had to be carried above the trailing axle - with an area of more than 40 square feet, it looked like there would be an awful lot of fire to feed.

Norman fired the first trip to show me the form and then it was my turn. Once I had learned the knack of getting the coal into the back corners, which required the shovel to be turned on edge and then through a right angle as it went through the firehole, I found the engine to be very free steaming and actually quite easy to fire. The up trip passed without incident, although the riding qualities of the engine were rather hard; so much so that my new tea can rattled itself off from the tray above the firehole and fell to the floor, putting a couple of large chips in the white enamel.

The return from Alton was a bit miserable, however: I had put on a big fire while standing at the station, making especially sure that the back corners were well filled. Norman obviously thought I had overdone it a bit and would not let me fire any more on the way back up the hill - every time I picked up the shovel he said not to fire, as we were still making a bit of smoke. Perhaps he thought that we would have enough to make it up without firing, or else he was trying to hammer home the smoke lesson, which I thought I already knew. Either way, the result was that we started to lose pressure over the last mile and eventually struggled over the top with about 150 pounds of steam and the water level uncomfortably low - Roger was looking pretty disgusted although he didn't say much and took us over the summit and into Medstead at walking pace to give the injectors time to refill the boiler. To make up for this lousy run, the next two round trips were real crackers, with both of us red-lining all the climbs, so the day came to an end with smiles all round.

The 29th June, 1995 is a day I shall always remember, as it was the first time I ever fired a Bulleid Pacific. In this case it was No. 34105 *Swanage*, one of the unrebuilt variety. Additionally, we had a numbers of VIPs, including the Lord Mayor of London and Ian Allan of the well-known publishing firm, travelling with us. Mike Burke, our driver, informed us that because of our distinguished visitors, it would be a seven coach train, two more than usual. In view of this and my recent experience on *Defiant*, when we nearly ran out of coal, I suggested to Mike that perhaps we should top up the tender - it takes pretty well a ton of coal just to light up one of these engines, which had made quite a dent on our supply already. Norman Batstone, the fireman, thought there should be enough but Mike agreed with me and tipped on another load, with our trusty, if somewhat battered, loading shovel. Thus prepared, we rumbled off shed and down to Alresford to pick up our train. It was a fine sunny day and on this light engine run, with the firedoors open, the very enclosed cab of No. 34105 was already turning into a hothouse.

At Alresford we coupled up to our train and Norman started to build up the fire. Norman was rather reticent about his age, but as he had been a pilot during the Berlin Airlift, it was not difficult to work out that he must be nearer 70 than 60 years old. As many men of his age would have difficulty just climbing up onto the footplate of *Swanage* from ground level, it was amazing that he could still perform a full firing turn and I had a great deal of admiration for him. On this occasion, however, he was not having a very good day and as we pulled out on our first trip, we had not gone very far before the boiler pressure began to drop. To compound the difficulty, we were running straight through at Ropley, so there would be no station stop to recover. We merely slowed down through the platform and I exchanged tokens, then Mike opened up again for the climb to Medstead. The pressure fell steadily all the way and nothing Norman did with the shovel seemed to improve it. After a couple of miles, the injector had to go on as well, which of course sent the clock back the wrong way even faster. Mike was nursing the engine as best he could to conserve steam and with Medstead station tantalisingly close, it looked as if we might make it. *Swanage*, however, had a rather poor brake ejector and when the pressure got down to about 150 psi, even though the engine was still pulling, the brakes came on and we ground to a halt about 100 yards short of the platform.

At this point, some readers may be wondering what sort of crazy system is it which allows the brakes to come on automatically even though the signals may be clear and the driver would prefer to keep going. To answer this question will now require the following short historical digression and a few technical details

In June 1889 an excursion train loaded with an incredible 940 passengers - most of them school children, left the station at Armagh in Northern Ireland, which is at the foot of a three mile gradient of around 1 in 75. The train consisted of 15 vehicles, which was two more than was allowed for the class of engine that was hauling it and the train eventually stalled on the gradient just short of the summit. The train was fitted with a non automatic form of the vacuum brake, in which air is admitted to the brakes to release them and a vacuum created to apply them (the opposite of the system in use today). With the train at a standstill, a decision was taken to divide it, so that the engine could take the first five vehicles over the top to a refuge siding and then return for the rest. As soon as the train was split between the fifth and sixth coaches, the brake would inevitably be released on all the vehicles in the rear, leaving only the guard's handbrake to hold the train on the gradient. Despite attempts to scotch the wheels with stones, this was not enough and the 10 coaches began to roll back down the hill at ever increasing speed. To make matters worse, the regular service train was now coming up the hill to meet the runaways, having been dispatched on the 'time interval' system - also now outlawed. In the ensuing terrible collision, 80 lives were lost - many of them being young children.

This was a defining moment in the history of railways, for a Bill was hastily rushed through Parliament which made it compulsory for passenger trains to be fitted with an automatic brake on all vehicles and for absolute block working to be introduced throughout the UK's railways - the latter ensuring that only one train was ever allowed into a section of line (block) on the same line at the same time.

The automatic vacuum brake, which is what concerns us here, is designed so that in the event of the train becoming divided due to a coupling failure, the brake pipes will also be torn apart and air will rush in and destroy the vacuum, thereby stopping both portions of the divided train. If you ever see a film where the hero (or villain, as the case may be) uncouples part of a moving passenger train and the front half continues running away, then you can impress your friends by asserting that it is all bull and telling them why.

Vacuum is usually measured in terms of the height of a column of mercury that can be hauled up a tube with the vacuum on top and atmospheric pressure beneath it. With a nearly perfect vacuum, atmospheric pressure which is just under 15 psi will support a mercury column of 30 in., so as a rule of thumb we can say that 2 in. of mercury is equivalent to 1 psi. The vacuum brake system that was in general use on British Railways operated at 21 in. of mercury except on ex-Great Western stock which used 25 in., which means that the maximum braking force available in a cylinder with 21 in. of vacuum on one side of the piston and full atmospheric pressure on the other is around 10 psi, (or 12 in the Great Western case). This is not a very big pressure and vacuum brake cylinders have to be given a very large diameter, so that there is enough piston area to develop the required braking force.

Apart from the vacuum brake cylinders, the other main parts of the system are the ejectors, which are there to create the vacuum in the first place, the driver's application valve which he uses to allow air to enter the system to apply the brakes and the train pipe, which conveys the vacuum from the locomotive down the train to all the brake cylinders. The guard on a passenger train also has an application valve and vacuum gauges so he too can apply the brake if required to do so.

Another requirement of the Act was that the passengers too would have a means of alerting the driver to an emergency so that he could stop the train - hence the introduction of the communication cord. This will not stop the train dead in its' tracks as many people believe but instead it will open a small air admission valve in the coach which will drop the vacuum enough to warn the driver, but not so much that he could not use the large ejector to blow the brake off again if he chose to do so; if for instance the train was going uphill in a tunnel, the driver would probably opt to drag the train out into the fresh air before stopping.

Compared to the injectors, the ejectors are very simple devices, consisting of little more than a steam jet squirting down a tube, which draws in the air from the train pipe behind it together with a couple of non return valves to prevent anything going back the wrong way. The exhaust steam and air are discharged into the smokebox and up the chimney. A vacuum relief valve is also fitted, which is there to prevent the vacuum rising above the required 21 inches. Normally, locomotives are fitted with two ejectors - a small one which is left on all the time to maintain the vacuum against minor leakages in the system, and a large one which may be used to 'blow the brakes off' quickly following station stops. The Great Western, which made a point of doing things differently, fitted a vacuum pump to one of the engine crossheads which would maintain the vacuum whilst running and did away with the small ejector.

By the time we had raised enough steam to blow the brakes off and continue, we were obviously running quite late and word had reached Ropley of our disgrace. When we got down to Alton, we found Dave Sibley waiting on the platform to take over the firing and Norman and I were booted unceremoniously into the guard's van while he set about catching up the lost time. He fired the next round trip from Alresford as well, while the VIPs were on board, before we were allowed back on the footplate. Dave decided that I should fire the first half of the next trip under his instructions and if he thought I was doing OK, would leave me to get on with it.

The grate is about the same size as on the 'Yank', but because it is carried above a trailing truck, instead of a coupled axle, the firebox can be made very much deeper at the back end and it is also much more steeply sloped down to the front. It is so deep in fact, that when I started making up the fire before departure, the first 50 shovels just seemed to disappear without trace. Dave exhorted me to keep on going. His advice was simple: 'Keep stuffing the back corners and under the doors until you think it's full, and then stuff it some more!' Following this procedure, I built up a huge U-shaped fire, thick across the back and tapering off down the sides towards the front. With this sort of preparation, once we got moving it was very easy to fire, with the coal being directed rather than thrown; the slope of the grate and the blast taking it to where it was required. The only difficulty that arose is when I tried to replenish the back corners, because the draft of air rushing through the firehole was so strong that it tended to drag the shovel inwards, so the coal finished up somewhere down the sides instead. However, I was keeping up the pressure quite happily and, true to his word, Dave got off at Alton and left me to it.

The first thing we had to do was to pull some more coal forwards, as despite the extra scoop that Mike put on earlier, it was already too far back in the tender to reach comfortably. Pulling coal down in a tender always seems to me to be harder work than actually throwing it on the fire. If you have somewhere to stand like the back of a 'Castle' or an 'S15' tender, then you can simply shovel it forward, although there will always be a certain amount of excavation required first before you get down to a flat surface to work off. On most engines however, the slope of the coal bunker ends in a vertical steel plate, so there is nowhere to slide the shovel in. In this case you have to stand at the coal face like a miner and claw it down with the coal pick, or maybe try and create a mini landslide by scrabbling it down with your boots. The pricker may also be employed as a kind of rake, which at least means that you can stand on the footplate while doing it, instead of having to climb into the tender (this is prohibited anyway if the engine is on the move). Whichever way you do it, it is bloody hard work and the pile you so laboriously bring down is soon dispatched into the fire and leaves you scratching for more. On this occasion, Norman, God bless him, pulled some down for me, while I re-stuffed the firebox in the approved Sibley fashion. That monster fire I had put on 10 miles back down the line had mostly now all gone and it took around 120 shovels to build it up again.

When the guard gave us the 'right away' Mike looked enquiringly in my direction to see if I was ready and upon receiving my somewhat uncertain thumbs up, gave a wail on the whistle and got *Swanage* away. I left the fire to burn through for the first half a mile and did nothing except to vary the firedoor opening to control the smoke, which Bulleid Pacifics can make in prodigious quantities. The boiler pressure began to rise as we passed the brewery and when it reached 245 I put on an injector. A little further on and the smoke had begun to clear so it was time to start firing again. I tried a pattern of about 8 shots, starting at one side and working round in a semi-circle to the other, then waited a few seconds for the smoke to clear again before repeating. *Swanage* seemed to thrive on this treatment and the pressure continued to hold against the injector. Mike showed he was no slouch on the regulator either and had the train accelerating rapidly up the 1 in 100 before the main climb started.

After the first mile there is a very short stretch of level track across the site of the former Butts Junction, where the old Basingstoke and Meon Valley lines used to branch off. This is in fact the only level section on the entire Railway and I took the opportunity to check the gauge glasses to see what the true water level was; on this occasion it was just bobbing in and out of sight at the top of the glass, which was fine, so it was back to the shovel again for the 1 in 60. A bit further on, between rounds of firing, I stole a quick glance at the speedometer; it was showing 36 mph, which with seven coaches on was not bad for an amateur!

We maintained this speed for the next mile or so until we passed the motocross track in Chawton Woods, at which point Mike told me I could pack up firing. Gratefully, I dropped the shovel, closed the firedoors and leant out of the window to cool off a bit while I listened to 'Swanage' purring away up the hill. When Medstead distant came into sight, I wound the damper closed, to allow the boiler pressure to fall a bit before Mike shut off steam at the summit. When he did so, the water level came back down to half a glass and I had to put on the second injector to prevent the engine from blowing off. I had held the boiler pressure against the injector all the way up the climb and when we reached the top we still had 230 psi and plenty of water, so I sat down feeling pretty pleased with myself.

For the remainder of the trip down to Alresford, I spent most of the time hanging out of the window in the slipstream trying to keep cool. It had turned out to be the hottest day of the year until then, with the temperature outside in the eighties, while the heat in the cab was almost unbearable - 130 at least. During 25 years as a Marine Engineer, I had been in ship's engine rooms that were as hot, but not in ones where you had to stand and work like a galley slave in front of a raging inferno. The trouble was that the big oval firedoor was open most of the time - on the downhill sections because you needed to keep the engine quiet and on the climbs because you had to stand in front of it to feed the beast, and there was nowhere in the cab that completely escaped the radiant heat.

When we arrived in Alresford the torment continued; first of all we needed another little excursion into the tender to bring more coal forward, then back to the footplate to throw the required 100 plus shovels into that insatiable furnace. In case you might think that this was overdoing it, I would point out that if you over-fired on the uphill sections, then the engine would blow off steam all down the other side, which would make you pretty unpopular with your driver. So far, the valves had only lifted once, so we must have been getting it about right.

One bit of good news was that we had shunted off two coaches for the last round trip, so the load was down to the usual five. I managed to fire the next leg back to Alton without problems, by which time I had definitely had enough and was more than happy to hand over the shovel to Norman for the final run back. That too passed off without incident and we could finally dispose of the engine and take our hot and weary bodies home. I don't think I had ever enjoyed a cold beer as much as I did that day. One other positive factor comes out of all this – the next time I checked my weight, I found I had lost half a stone since the beginning of the year!

The last turn I shall describe in this chapter occurred in October 1995 with Mike Burke again as driver and Neil Davies as fireman. When I arrived in the morning and checked the board for the engine number, it was No. 73096, which was fast becoming my favourite, so I looked forward to an enjoyable day. Neil was supposed to be taking his firing test, so we expected Bob Deeth to put in an appearance at some time. He duly turned up about half an hour before we were due to go off shed and said he would observe Neil fire the first round trip after which he wanted to see me have a go as well, which did my nerves no good at all.

We ran down to Alresford and Bob watched Neil couple up the train, which is one of the other things a fireman is supposed to know about. This is a lot more difficult than it looks and needs a bit of practice to become proficient. The main thing to remember is to let go the vacuum pipes first when unhooking and to leave the ends dangling; this way the brakes will remain hard on and nothing can move. Next to go is the steam heating pipe, not forgetting to shut off the cocks on engine and tender before so doing, if you want to avoid an unexpected blast of steam; finally unscrew the coupling to get some slack and heave it off the hook. When coupling up, everything is done in reverse order, coupling first, then steam heat and finally the vacuum pipe. Now letting go the vacuum pipes is the easy bit, but getting them back together is quite another story and the first time I tried it was like wrestling with a couple of reluctant anacondas. The secret is to angle them apart so that the 'horns' go in first, after which the two slotted bars should engage fairly easily; finally insert one of the spring clips through the slots to prevent them undoing again.

Neil managed this little chore without difficulty, however, and in due course we got the 'right away' and departed on the first leg. Neil soon had the engine steaming beautifully but was a little slow to get the injector on when we shut off steam for Ropley and the safety valves lifted, which earned him a black mark.

The next section up to Medstead also went pretty well but there was a bit of drizzle coming down and the engine developed wheel slip a few times in the cutting before the station. This had me wondering about how we would fare on the more difficult return climb from Alton. These damp mornings leave a thin film of slimy rust on the railhead which always causes more adhesion problems than when it is raining hard. We have sanding gear on the locomotives but it is seldom used as it is difficult to maintain and can cause additional wear and tear if it gets into places it shouldn't.

Sure enough, when we left Alton, the engine suffered intermittent bouts of slipping almost from the start and Mike had not managed to get the speed up to 25 mph by the time we reached Butts bridge. From then on as the gradient steepened, things got progressively worse and Mike's arm got plenty of exercise as he opened and closed the regulator to control the spinning wheels. By the time we reached the race track, we were almost down to walking pace and I was convinced we would stall. Bob Deeth, however, had a little trick up his sleeve which got us out of trouble. The steam brake on No. 73096 operates on both the engine and tender wheels, but there is an isolating cock at the foot of the brake pedestal that shuts off the steam to the tender. Bob bent down and closed this valve, which meant that Mike could now leave the regulator open as much as the engine would take and if a slip did occur, it could be arrested by the steam brake, which was now working on the engine wheels only. By this method, the power was being applied with less interruption and very slowly we gained speed and dragged ourselves over the summit, which incidentally, at 652 feet above sea level, is the highest point reached by any railway in Southern England.

At the very top of the climb, the cutting is spanned by a tall and impressive brick overbridge that carries the road from Medstead up to the A31 at Four Marks. Generations of tired enginemen struggling up the gradient have looked out for this marker because it meant that their ordeal was over, hence it is commonly, if somewhat irreverently known as 'Thank Christ Bridge'. As it is very difficult to manage a fire when an engine is slipping like we were, I was quite sure that Neil would have approved of the name, especially as he was under Bob's critical gaze. Bob was obviously satisfied with his efforts, however, as he now indicated it was my turn to have a go.

During the downhill run to Alresford, there was nothing much for me to do, beyond answering a few of Bob's questions, which I managed without difficulty; no doubt my job as a boiler inspector and previous steam experience on board ship spared me a more searching examination.

I fired the return run to Alton fairly well but Bob showed me a couple of useful tips which I have used ever since. The first thing he told me was to let go of the shovel handle at the point of delivery when making long shots - not completely of course but just with the leading hand! This allows the blade to fully enter the firebox, which reduces the distance you need to throw and also gets the coal past any hump inside the firedoor. The second tip concerned footwork; up to then I had always maintained a stance halfway between tender and firehole and never moved the feet when firing. Bob's method was to stand much more upright and take a small step toward the tender with one foot to load the shovel and then pivot round and step back toward the fire to make the shot; the other foot remained stationary. This method made for a lot less bending and twisting from the waist and also meant that the throw didn't need to be so hard, as the body was already moving toward the fire with the shovel. Bob said that when you had to do it every day for a living, the whole idea was to make the job as easy as possible and watching him perform was quite an education, as he never seemed to be putting in any effort at all.

When we made the return run from Alton, I had been a bit slow in making up the fire and at departure time we only had 210 lb. of steam and three-quarters of a glass of water. As it was essential to have a full glass before shutting off at the top, it meant the injector had to go on pretty well from the word go and had to stay on all the way up. Fortunately, the exhaust injector on No. 73096 was a particularly good one and the feed could be throttled in to match the engine's demand for steam; this had the further advantage of a pre-heating the water a bit more before it entered the boiler.

I fired steadily all the way up to the racetrack, five or six shovels at a time, pausing briefly between rounds to allow the smoke to clear. At this stage I could have done with some small coal or dust to fire over the flap, which would have kept the pressure up a bit longer without leaving too big a fire at the top. All I had left however were large lumps, so I closed the firedoors and sat down instead. At the summit the pressure was down to 180 psi but I had the necessary full glass of water, so things could have been worse. This was one of the many manifestations of Sod's Law, which stated that however well you might perform without an audience, as soon as a footplate inspector was there to stand behind you, things would invariably go down the drain!

A few days after this when I was working in the shed, I happened to mention this little episode to John Bunch, who was then in charge of the locomotive department and said that I didn't think I had done very well. His reply took me completely by surprise, however, when he said, 'You don't have to worry, Bob thinks you're a natural'. Coming as it had from a former main line driver, this remark left me feeling 10 feet tall.

Some weeks later when I was checking the crew lists for the following year, I found that despite having only completed 12 trips as third man, I was now marked up as a fireman, so I was one step further up the ladder.

Chapter Five

Black Prince, 'Thomas' and the 'U Boat'

After the 'Santa Specials' are finished, there are not many scheduled services on the Railway for a couple of months, so I had to wait until early March 1996 for my first turn as rostered fireman. My regular crew now consisted of driver Jim Lawrence who was one of the full time staff, with Martin Butler as third man. Later on when Bob Deeth took over in charge of the locomotive department, the term 'third man' was dropped and 'cleaner' adopted instead, which made it more like the old railway system. Martin had accrued considerably more footplate turns than me but for some reason seemed happy enough to remain as cleaner. I was a little concerned at first that he might feel aggrieved that I had been promoted ahead of him, but if that was the case, he never showed it and it suited me well enough to have someone with me who knew what he was doing and didn't need any instruction. Later on, when I was attempting to train less experienced cleaners, I found it was a lot harder than actually doing the job yourself, so I take this opportunity to thank the two Normans and my other mentors for putting up with me when I was learning the trade.

Upon arriving in the 'Manor', I checked the board to see which engine I would have for my maiden firing turn - and what an engine it was - BR Standard '9F' No. 92203, now called *Black Prince*. Apart from a few Garratts (articulated engines with power bogies at each end and the boiler in the middle) on the LMS and London & North Eastern Railway (LNER), these were the biggest freight engines ever employed in this country. Apart from their heavy haulage capabilities, they had also acquired quite a reputation for fast running on passenger trains, when an express engine had been unavailable.

This particular '9F' is owned by the popular artist David Shepherd, who is famous particularly for his elephant pictures but is better known amongst the railway fraternity for his series of paintings at Nine Elms and other engine sheds during the final months of steam on the Southern. For me, David Shepherd has captured exactly the feelings of despair and waste that accompanied the last days of main line steam, when all that had been so carefully built up over the previous hundred and more years was so recklessly discarded, virtually overnight, by the faceless accountants who ran British Railways. David Shepherd himself was obviously so moved by what he saw, that he promptly went out and bought himself two steam locomotives and saved them from the scrap men. These engines were the '9F' as noted above and BR Standard class '4' 4-6-0 No. 75029 which he called *The Green Knight*.

And was this 'Brave New World' of diesel and electric traction such a great leap forward? Did we all eagerly anticipate a train journey any more than before? I think not. The main differences that I could see were firstly, that with the wholesale closures of stations and branch lines, there were now a lot fewer places you could actually go to by train and secondly, that we had lost that wonderful steam engine aroma in exchange for stinking diesel fumes, which

Superpower at Ropley. David Shepherd's '9F' class No 92203 *Black Prince* stands in front of sister engine No. 92212.

R. Forster

can be had in any traffic jam. Well OK then, so what's wrong with electric traction; that at least is pollution free isn't it? I'm afraid not. All we have done here is to transfer the locomotive exhaust to the power station chimney and every time the driver of an electric train opens the power handle, another dollop of greenhouse gas goes up into the atmosphere (unless of course it's a nuclear power station). Ironically, even in 2005 when I eventually finished this book, it is more than likely that the power station prime mover is still a steam turbine!

There is also the question of visual pollution to consider. The image of a steam train puffing across the landscape is a pleasure to many and somehow seems to blend in but even if you can't stand the sight of the things, when the train has passed the scene of rural tranquillity returns. With electric traction however, the overgrown cat's cradle of catenary wire, insulators and support gantries marching across the country is an eyesore to everyone and never goes away.

Having aired my somewhat jaundiced opinions of modern railways, I would hasten to add that all the trains I have travelled on recently have been quiet, comfortable and fast - even though there may no longer be a window to lower on a leather strap, so that you can hang out to spot the ¼ mileposts!

Returning to 'Ropley Manor' once again, I signed on and started to read the notices. Before commencing any turn of duty, it is essential to read these, so you will know about temporary speed restrictions, water availability and the like. The previous driver's report card will also be studied, to see if there are any defects to watch out for on the engine. On this occasion there was nothing of any consequence on the report card but a note on the board caught my eye, stating that the engine was not to be cleaned, as it was required for filming purposes and had to look authentically dirty; that was fine by me as it meant one less chore to perform.

After unlocking the shed and collecting the rags and paraffin for lighting up, I walked outside and found the engine standing in the yard instead of over the pit. Seen thus from ground level, instead of from the height of the coal stage, the locomotive looked to be a very powerful brute, with the small driving wheels accentuating the bulk of the huge boiler.

Throwing up my shovel onto the footplate, together with the leather bag containing my lunch and the rule book, plus a bucket of tools and my tea can, all of which were by now my usual footplate accessories, I mounted the steps and surveyed the cab. Apart from the width of the boiler facing me, everything was almost identical to the 'Standard 5', so I felt at home almost immediately. A look into the firebox showed a grate that was roughly the same size as on *Swanage* but very much shallower and with only a slight slope toward the front. This is because the grate and ashpan have to be carried above the rearmost coupled axle, instead of the trailing truck arrangement on the Bulleid engine, which is considerably lower. The '9Fs' were undoubtedly the finest heavy freight engine to run on British Railways, and if they had any deficiencies at all, then the ashpan, which was also quite shallow and therefore of small capacity, was it. For my part though, I was happy enough to see the shallower grate, because it would obviously require a lot less shovelling to fill it!

The usual checks for water and steam showed we had three-quarters of a glass and 40 lb. of steam, so there would be plenty of time for preparation. After operating the rocking grate and knocking as much of the residues as possible through the gaps with the fire irons, there was still a fair bit left in the corners which are difficult to reach, so I decided to get in the firebox and clear it by hand. I always reckon that if you start the day with a thoroughly clean fire, then you are giving yourself the best chance of completing the turn without steaming troubles.

When I was at sea, it was quite often necessary to get in the furnace side of boilers which still had some steam pressure and providing you took sensible precautions, like ensuring your mate was standing by the door in case you got in trouble, there was really nothing to it. With a locomotive, the first job is remove the deflector plate with the shovel blade and then put on a face mask to avoid inhaling the dust. The blower should be cracked on slightly which will draw some fresh air in through the door. I always go in feet first and face down, which means that you can feel the heat on your legs before you get all the way in and can decide whether to chicken out or not. In this case, it seemed OK, so I extended my arms straight out above my head and wriggled in the rest of the way. Once inside, it took only a few minutes work with the shovel to scrape the remaining ash and clinker down into the ashpan.

Sometimes you may find a few stubborn bits of clinker adhering to the fire bars; these can usually be whacked off with whatever tool comes to hand - a nice meaty spanner from the tool locker usually does the trick. While in the box you can also take a good look at the tubeplate to check for leaks and to remove any clinker 'bird nests' that may be blocking the tube ends. If you are feeling really keen, the ash can be shovelled down from the top of the brick arch as well, although I would normally only bother to do this if it was up to the bottom rows of tubes.

The temperature may be as much as 150 degrees Fahrenheit (65 Celsius) in a firebox like this, which no doubt has many readers thinking I am a bit of a 'line shooter' but I can assure you that it is true and neither am I Superman. The reason you can withstand such temperatures, for short periods at least, is that the humidity is almost down to zero, which means that your perspiration evaporates almost instantly and keeps your body temperature within limits. I once served on a ship called the *Esso Durham* which was a steam turbine-driven oil tanker. In the boiler room the temperature on the 'plates' (the operating position down at the bottom level) was normally in the 110 to 120 range, when the ship was in tropical waters, but the higher you climbed up the boilers the hotter it got. Once a day it was necessary to go right up to the exhaust uptake level some 40 ft higher, to take samples of the flue gas for analysis. There was a thermometer hanging on the hand rail up there (too hot to touch without gloves) and on one occasion in the Persian Gulf, when I went to take the sample it was registering 168 degrees Fahrenheit. This was the highest temperature I ever experienced at sea and needless to say I didn't hang around up there very long!

Now I had done my stint in the firebox, Martin checked the chimney end and then it was time to light the fire. I spread a layer of coal over the entire grate in the usual way, saving all the bigger lumps for the back corners and under the firedoor. Then the wood and paraffin-soaked rags went down under the brick arch and finally a bit more coal was thrown in on top to complete the job. I had one last decent sized piece of rag, which I placed in the shovel and ceremoniously lit up - the first time I had applied the magic match myself. When it was blazing nicely, I gave it a good swing and chucked it in the firebox, only to have it catch on the brick arch and hang there like a burning curtain! I had to resort to hooking it down with a fire iron, by which time it had nearly gone out anyway and I had to search around for another bit to repeat the process. After this minor embarrassment, I no longer use the shovel method, preferring instead to save a stick of wood to wrap the rag round and then throw it in by hand, which is a lot more accurate.

The brick arch incidentally, is a feature to be found on all nearly standard gauge engines but rarely on narrow gauge ones or road engines. It is in fact an arch as described, made of firebricks or other refractory material and is erected in the firebox like a roof over the front half of the fire. The front abuts against the tubeplate just below the bottom row of tubes and the edges rest on studs projecting from the firebox side plates. The whole thing is inclined upwards from front to back to match the slope of the grate, or possibly steeper. Without the arch, the burning coals at the front of the firebox would only be a foot or so below the tubes and could be sucked straight through and shot up the chimney when the engine was working hard. Apart from setting fire to the surrounding countryside, this would be a considerable waste of fuel. The arch prevents this from happening and the much longer flame travel that results allows the combustible gases emanating from the coal time to burn off before passing down the tubes, thereby improving the thermal efficiency of the boiler.

Now we had finally lit the fire, Martin and I decided we should at least make a thorough job of cleaning the cab, if not the rest of the engine, while Jim pottered round with the oil cans and attended to the lubrication requirements. After we had been at this task for half an hour or so, we heard a shout from below and looked out to see David Shepherd himself standing by the cab - and not looking very happy. He demanded to know why his engine was so filthy, so we explained about the no cleaning notice in the 'Manor', which did little to placate him. It seemed that someone had got their wires a bit crossed; the filming part was correct but David said that the intention was to have the engine 'made up' and he certainly didn't want real dirt!

After this little bombshell, we did our best in the remaining time to at least give the boiler and motion a wipe over, while David himself got out the 'Brassso' and polished up the 'Black Prince' name plates.

By the time we had run down to Alresford and started playing trains, David had cheered up, however, so I asked him if he wanted to have a go on the shovel. This offer he declined, with the comment that we would finish up with more coal on the cab floor than in the firebox. I didn't really believe this was very likely and thought instead that he was just being a gentleman, by allowing us to make the most of what may have been our only outing on his engine.

Although we only had a five-coach train, which was a piffling load for such a powerful locomotive, both Martin and myself were finding it quite difficult to fire and steam was by no means as easy to come by as we would have liked. Once again, a badly burnt and distorted deflector plate in the firehole was the problem. This was drooping down at the front and tended to catch the coal as it went past, causing it to drop short and form a hump in the fire that further compounded the difficulty. Unlike *Swanage*, where the grate is steeply-sloped and therefore virtually self feeding, providing you can keep the back end filled up, this flatter grate needed firing all over, so we were tending to starve the front of fuel. I tried wedging small pieces of coal between the deflector plate flange and the firehole rim to tilt it up a bit, but they didn't stay put very long.

After a couple of mediocre trips we were both feeling a bit downcast at our lack of success and just to make things worse, Bob Deeth appeared to see how we were getting on. After hearing our tale of misfortune, Bob took the shovel to give us a demonstration while Martin and I stood back to watch. Neither of us were really expecting him to do much better and were quietly satisfied to note that even he couldn't throw the coal down the front either. Bob, however, remained completely relaxed and just continued piling coal in wherever it would go, making the hump even bigger, while the clock continued to subside. After this he simply got down the pricker from the tender, pushed the heap around to where he wanted it and then stood back to await results. Within a couple of minutes that pressure gauge was back on the red line and we had to put an injector on to avoid blowing off! This performance left the two of us feeling suitable humbled but with another 'trick of the trade' stored up in the memory banks. Bob told us later that deflector plates on '9Fs' were a common problem in BR days and that in certain depots which had a large allocation of these engines, piles of discarded plates could often be found in some deserted corner of the shed where frustrated firemen had 'lost them'. Having shown us how to do it, Bob left us to get on with it and I am pleased to report that we finished the day on a high note with a cracking final run up from Alton.

Having completed this turn on one of the largest engines to run on the Mid-Hants, the next was by contrast, on 'Thomas', which is the smallest of our resident stable. As I mentioned in Chapter Three, 'Thomas' was originally a 'J94' 'Austerity' saddle tank locomotive built by the Hunslet Engine Company sometime around World War II. The word 'Austerity' indicated the wartime origins of the design, which was intended to be produced as cheaply and quickly as possible, so there were no frills such as wheel splashers or decorative brass beading around the cab windows. Many of these engines survived into the preservation era because they had operated on industrial sites, outside the control of British Railways. Their owners included the coal, gas and electricity Boards who did not consider it a number one priority to cut up steam engines in the way that BR did and were happy to sell them on into private hands, where they formed the original motive power for quite a number of railway preservation schemes. This was especially true in the early days, before any of the wrecks from Dai Woodham's scrapyard on Barry Island had been restored.

Checking in my Ian Allan *Combined Volume* for 1958/9, the data for the engine shows the remarkable tractive effort of 23,870 lb., which is almost identical to our 'U' class 2-6-0. This has been achieved by having large cylinders and small wheels, which means in effect that it is very low geared. Tractive effort, however, can be a very misleading parameter by which to compare locomotive performance and is simply the pulling force that can be applied at the rails. It takes no account of boiler capacity or the adhesion weight of the engine. Express engines, therefore, can often exert a greater force than the friction with the rails will allow, which may lead to bouts of wheel slip, especially on starting. Shunting engines like this, on the other hand, where all the weight is available for adhesion, are usually very sure footed. Put one an express train, however, and you will immediately face a different problem. Because they are designed for short trips, their boiler capacity is not very great and the cylinders can actually gobble the steam faster than the boiler can produce it, so they will quickly become short of breath if any sustained effort to run at speed is required. The trip up from Alresford to Ropley with four coaches therefore, becomes quite a challenge if it is to be run to the same schedule as the bigger engines. However, on this occasion, our duties for the day only involved playing with the 'Troublesome Trucks' in Ropley yard for the entertainment of the children, so our steam requirements would be minimal.

Having signed on in the 'Manor' and collected the usual accoutrements from the shed, I made my way down to the engine, which was standing on the pit road between 'James' and the 'Standard 5'. Climbing aboard to take stock, the main impression was how terribly cramped the cab was, compared to the tender engines I had become used to. There was definitely no room to swing the proverbial cat - nor a shovel either from what I could see! My own shovel is one of a batch brought back from South Africa by Clive Holiday, one of our permanent staff who has fired and driven out there. It is a bit smaller than a Great Western shovel but a very solid tool nonetheless, made from a heavy gauge steel pressing with a very stout wooden handle, suitable for Clive no doubt - or even possibly a mountain gorilla! To make it a more nimble weapon, I have trimmed about an inch off the blade all round the edges and taken a spokeshave to the woodwork, so that it fits my delicate little paws rather better. It was still to big for 'Thomas' however, so I fell back on my old Aveling & Porter steam roller shovel, which is about a foot shorter.

Another disagreeable feature of the cab, is the number of pipes and valves that encroach into the already limited space, all capable of burning the unwary hand or arm that strays too close. This is a shame, because although 'Thomas' is very popular with the children, it is unsafe to have more than one at a time on the footplate and then only under the strictest supervision. The 'Standard 5' by contrast can take three or four and providing they sit on the seats or stand by the tender, there is nothing within easy reach on which they can hurt themselves.

While I had been grubbing around in the cab attending to the fire lighting, Jim Lawrence had turned up and commenced his oiling up routines. No doubt when the engine was in its original saddle tank form, this procedure was a lot easier than it is now because the driver would have been able to reach most of the oiling points from the running plate. The new side tanks, however, were copied from the 'Thomas' books with appearance rather than accessibility in mind, so Jim had to do a fair bit of clambering around underneath to get at them all - in fact it takes considerably longer to oil up 'Thomas' than it does the 'Standard 5'.

Martin Butler had now arrived and seeing as I had done all the dirty work of fire lighting, I had no pangs of conscience about sending him down into the pit to rake out the ashpan. This particular chore is ideal for those who would aspire to that pale complexion reminiscent of portraits of Queen Elizabeth I. The fine white ash adheres beautifully to hot sweaty faces and this is one of those jobs where you can guarantee that the wind will always be blowing toward you!

With the preparation completed, the finishing touch was to give 'Thomas's' face a good clean before lifting it up and securing it to the smokebox door. Although 'Thomas' is the smallest engine, it has the biggest face, being the full diameter of the smokebox and it was quite a tricky job teetering about on the front plating while trying to manoeuvre it into position. But Martin and I managed the task without dropping either the face or ourselves into the pit and wandered back to the 'Manor' for the usual pot of tea, which could be taken at leisure because we had to wait for the other engines to move off before we were required.

When we eventually had a clear road, we trundled down the yard and marshalled our train, which consisted of a few wagons and a brake van. Our job for the day was to provide a spectacle for the visitors on the grassy bank behind the up platform, where a refreshment marquee and picnic area had been set up. This site gives a good view of the whole of Ropley station and yard and, with a four-train service, there is a movement every few minutes. The 'Fat Controller' strides the platform, while a commentator uses the public address system to let everyone know what is going on. We used every possible permutation of movements we could, in the limited space available, to re-enact scenes from the 'Thomas' books. These included 'Thomas with boiler ache', where we pretended to have a problem by blowing steam from the injector overflow pipes and then caught 'fish' from the side tanks to cure it. Then there was 'Thomas in a hurry', where someone quietly uncoupled the wagons and we steamed off rapidly and left them behind. We also had races with other departing trains, where we started from the down platform and ran up the pit road, while the service train left at the same time from the up side. This meant we could run alongside each other for a couple of hundred yards, which gave time for the lead to change hands several times and was quite exciting for the spectators on the bank.

No doubt some of the visiting 'enthusiasts' looked down their noses at these little games but the children all loved it and will hopefully come again, which made our job just as important as running the service trains with the bigger engines. From the firing point of view, the work was hardly very demanding and all that was required was a few shovels now and again to keep the grate covered, taking care not to overdo it and allow the safety valves to lift at inopportune moments, which would drown out the public address.

Having completed this turn at the Easter 'Thomas' event in 1996, it was another three years before I found myself rostered for the engine again, only this time we were going to be running a shuttle service to and from Alresford, so it would be a bit more of a challenge. I was paired up with driver Geoff Bailey for this turn, who told me we were going to bring the empty stock up from Alresford first and then run six shuttles there and back, making seven runs up the bank in total - more than enough for a day's work.

Having prepared the engine and run down to Alresford to collect our four-coach train, I made a start building up the fire. One problem I hadn't bargained for was the size of the coal. Given the nature of the line, we are normally supplied with good grade coal of decent size and without too much slack. This particular batch however, had quite a few really large lumps in amongst it, some of which must have weighed around 40 lb. These would be fine for the back corners of the grate on *Swanage*, where the only criteria is whether or not they would go through the firehole. 'Thomas' however, liked his food in smaller mouthfuls, which meant that all the big lumps would have to be broken up before firing (several small pieces will burn a lot quicker than one big one). The opening from the footplate into the coal bunker could also get blocked up every so often, if a particularly large boulder came down; needless to say this would invariably happen when you needed to put some on in a hurry. The effect of all this coal bashing, was that the cab floor was always in a mess and was a further discouragement to footplate visitors, who have to be kept clear of the flying shrapnel as you wield the coal pick.

As there was no particular worry about departure time on this empty stock run, I could afford the luxury of building the fire right up and having a full head of steam and a full glass of water before we left, so the first trip turned out quite well. After we got going, 'Thomas' barked noisily as he got stuck into the 1 in 80, the small wheels giving rapid fire exhaust beats which made you think you were going a lot faster than you really were. I waited a minute or so to give the fire a chance to get really hot before I started firing. Then it was a case of whipping open the doors with the left hand, throw in a quick shovel shot, close them again, reload the shovel and repeat. I had taken the precaution of giving all the runners and pivots of the door mechanism a good oiling beforehand, so the doors opened and closed as sweetly as possible. With this treatment the pressure was just about holding but after the first mile, the injector had to go on and thereafter it declined slowly. By the time we got in sight of Ropley home signal and Geoff shut off, it was down to 150 psi which was about right, as this was only 20 lb. below the red line on this engine and we didn't want to be standing in Ropley yard blowing off steam from the safeties.

The quality of the remaining trips turned out to be pretty much determined by the sort of preparation you made - if you had a full pot and full head of steam to start with, things would be OK. If however you had left things a bit late and had to depart with perhaps 160 psi and half a glass, then it would be tight - I was down to 120 psi on one of my runs with only an inch of water, but we made it nonetheless.

Each time we arrived in Ropley, we unhooked straight away and ran off down the pit road until we cleared the points and could then drop back toward the shed, whereupon our diesel shunter drew the train forward for us up to the other end of the pit road. This procedure meant that the platform loop and running line were quickly cleared to allow the service trains to cross. Our coaches were now obstructing our access to the water column, so each time we arrived we took a squirt from a firehose instead, to keep our tanks topped up. Having given 'Thomas' a drink, we ran forward again and hooked onto our train again ready for the next trip, and so it went on. Although we may not have covered many miles, it had been non-stop activity all day and we were as black as crows into the bargain. What with all the coal breaking and the horrible

The 'Fat Controller' and Bob Deeth playing trains at Ropley.

Author/© 2008 Gullane (Thomas) Ltd

The 'Governor' - Mr Bob Deeth, Locomotive Superintendent of the Mid-Hants Railway, helps to clean 'Thomas'.

Author/© 2008 Gullane (Thomas) Ltd

'James the Red Engine' alias 'U' class 2-6-0 No. 31625.

P. Goodworth

cramped cab to work in, not helped by having to keep one's jacket on to avoid getting burnt, little 'Thomas' had turned out to be a hard day's work - give me a big engine any day!

Our 'U' class 2-6-0 No. 31625, which had been undergoing restoration in the workshop from its' scrapyard state, was finally completed in the late summer of 1996 and I eagerly looked forward to getting a turn on it. This occurred a few weeks later with driver Barry Eden and Martin Butler as cleaner. Having completed the usual formalities in the 'Manor', we wandered out to the yard and found the engine standing over the pit, looking absolutely splendid in its' lined black BR livery. The cab too was in wonderfully clean condition and it was still possible to discern the original colour of the wooden floorboards under the ingrained coal dust.

Compared with 'James' which is an 'N' class, the 'U' is almost identical apart from the driving wheels, which are 6 ft diameter against 5 ft 6 in. for the 'N'. Referring to my Ian Allan 'bible' once again, it tells me that the 'N' was introduced first in 1917, whilst the 'U' did not appear until 1928. Both have two outside cylinders and 200 psi boilers with Belpaire (flat top) fireboxes. It is quite possible that the first engine I ever saw was one of these two classes, as they ranged all over the Southern Region, including East Croydon, where my father first took me as a small child.

The engine has all the usual 'mod cons' such as rocking grates and drop doors on the ashpan, which make the preparation a straightforward job, although I still carried out my normal firebox inspection from the inside and cleared away the remaining ash and clinker. There were one or two bigger pieces that would not drop down through the fire bars, so I passed them out through the firehole for Martin to dispose of. The coal looked like our usual decent stuff from one of the Scottish pits, so I was a little surprised to see so much clinker and hoped it would not adversely affect the steaming as the day progressed.

By the time we had lit the fire at around 7 am the weather had taken a turn for the worse and rain was coming down, so we confined our cleaning activities to the wheels and motionwork, where we could stay under the relative shelter of the running plate. After a while, though, the rain got heavier, so we retired to the cab and cowered under the storm sheet. This is basically just a tarpaulin fixed onto hooks around the edge of the cab roof at the front and by elastic ties to the tender at the rear. This provides a reasonable degree of protection from the elements and is certainly quite luxurious compared with generations of the early engines, which didn't even have a full cab roof until around 1900.

By 8 am the fire was burning nicely and had worked its way back up the grate toward the firehole, while the pressure, which was 30 psi when we arrived, had now finally started to rise. This first hour after the fire is lit never does much for the pressure and I often used to worry about having enough steam to be able to move off at the right time. But it is amazing how quickly the pressure will rise, once the fire is burning all over the grate and there is enough steam to work the blower. On this occasion, there was 60 lb. of steam on the clock at 8.30 when we went off for our morning tea, having left the blower just cracked open but on our return less than half an hour later it was up to 140 and rising fast.

'James the Red Engine' except that this time he's black! 'U' class 2-6-0 No. 31625 approaches Ropley. *Author/© 2008 Gullane (Thomas) Ltd*

My old friend Peter Goodworth shows he is no slouch on the shovel as he fires No. 31625 in 1999. *P. Goodworth*

Today, we were picking up our train from the Alton end, so I carried on building up the fire a bit more, especially at the back end, so we would be ready for the uphill section to Medstead. When we ran down to the box to collect the token the rain had eased off again to a fine drizzle, but the rails were very slippery and even on this light engine run we suffered a few bouts of wheel slip in the cutting before Medstead station. This did not bode very well for the return trip and sure enough, after we ran down to Alton and coupled up to the stock, we had considerable difficulty dragging it of the siding and past the roadbridge, before we could let it gravitate back into the platform. This at least provided the waiting passengers with some unscheduled entertainment, as they watched us slipping and sliding' while Barry heaved the regulator open and shut.

When we got the green flag, we experienced more slipping until the engine was over the pointwork and out onto the running line. Thereafter things improved slightly and Barry managed to get the train up to about 25 mph by the time we reached Butts Junction. As soon as we hit the 1 in 60 though, the slipping occurred more and more frequently and we steadily lost speed. Barry tried all possible combinations of regulator, cut-off and brake to arrest the spinning wheels but the engine never seemed to grip for more than a few yards at a time. The climb up to 'Thank Christ' bridge seemed interminable and at one point I was convinced we would slip to a stand, while Martin was even getting ready to jump down with the bucket and hand sand the rail. Somehow Barry managed to keep the engine moving, though, and eventually we dragged ourselves over the summit and rolled down into Medstead nearly 15 minutes late.

After this drama, the rest of the trip passed without incident and a quick turn round at Alresford even had us back on time again for the next service. I have found that it is nearly always the case that any slipping trouble will occur on the first trip of the day, after which, even though it may continue to rain, the slimy rust has been polished off by the passing wheels and the locomotives seem to able to hold their feet. This turned out to be the case today and we had no further slipping problems, so we could all relax a bit and start to enjoy the engine, which was steaming superbly. The boiler was such a good steam raiser that both Martin and I were tending to over-fire a bit and were actually finding it harder to keep the engine quiet than to make steam. On one occasion, while we were waiting in Alresford , I had to resort to poking a hole in the middle of the fire with the pricker to make sure we didn't lift the safety valves in the station. This little ploy means that all the air entering the ashpan will take the line of least resistance up through the bare fire bars, instead of through the burning coals, so the fire will die right down. It is important when doing this, to ensure that the hole does not extend right up to the firebox sides, otherwise the cold air hitting a localised area of the plating could cause some uneven contraction of the metal, which might cause a stay or two to leak, or possibly even start a crack in the plate which would mean a very expensive repair.

With less than five minutes to go, I got the pricker down again from the tender and pushed and pulled the fire around to fill the hole then threw some fresh coal down the sides and under the door to complete the rebuilding process. When we got going, Barry opened the regulator and the locomotive strode purposefully away up the gradient, showing impressive acceleration and with a lovely crisp exhaust beat. I whacked a half dozen shots down to the front of the box when Barry notched up and was immediately rewarded by a plume of smoke from the funnel. This soon cleared, which was the engine telling me that it needed feeding again, so I shot another three down each side and two down the middle - Norman style. Despite the unorthodox preparation with the fire looking half dead just before we started, the boiler was soon producing steam faster than we could use it and I needed to put on an injector to avoid blowing off. When Ropley distant appeared and Barry shut off, I needed the second one as well but was a bit slow in getting it on, so the safeties lifted violently as we ran down the platform. Fortunately, the rain had kept the usual audience inside the shed, so only the signalman and the station staff were there to witness my mistake.

After the final run of the day, when we had parked the coaches back in the siding once again, Barry stepped across to my side of the footplate and told me to drive the engine back to Ropley. This took me rather by surprise, as I had never been offered the regulator before by my regular driver. Maybe he did this with all his firemen, or perhaps it was because it was now throwing it down with rain and it meant that I would be the one with his head stuck outside the cab getting soaked instead of him! Either way, I was quite happy to have a go and managed to get us back to the shed without too much difficulty.

Having given the boiler a blowdown at the top end of the pit road, we moved down to the coal stage, which required no more than a quick puff of steam to get us rolling, after which gravity did the rest. Dave Sibley hand-signalled me forward to get the locomotive positioned right for coaling and I managed to stop pretty well on the exact spot - whereupon he told me to go back six inches! Cursing under my breath, I was just about to start winding the engine into reverse for this delicate little shunt when I saw that he was kidding, so I politely told him to get stuffed and secured the engine instead - regulator closed, reverser in mid-gear, cylinder cocks open and tender handbrake on. Martin chocked the wheels and then we carried out all the usual disposal duties before retiring to the 'Manor' for a brew and to sign off.

No. 31625 had turned out to be a really good locomotive and was ideally suited to our line, being more economical than the bigger engines but still having plenty of power in hand when hauling our normal five- or six-coach trains. Regrettably, the boiler developed problems after only a few years in service and the engine is now one of several parked up at the back of the running shed awaiting its turn in the repair queue - and at the time of publication is still waiting!

Chapter Six

Bulleid Pacifics - The Science Bit

Oliver Bulleid was chief mechanical engineer of the Southern Railway from 1937 until Nationalisation in 1948. When he took over the reins from Robert Maunsell, he inherited a very wide variety of motive power but only a handful of top line express passenger engines - these being the 16 'Lord Nelson' class 4-6-0s. Although they were powerful machines, capable of hauling the heaviest trains then timetabled on the Southern, they were also rather complex and expensive to maintain, with four sets of valve gear and had a very long firebox, which was tricky to fire. Additionally there were the 49 'King Arthur' 4-6-0s, which were strong and reliable but not exactly speedy and the 40 three-cylinder 'Schools' class 4-4-0s, which were excellent locomotives but rather prone to slipping - having a considerably lower percentage of adhesion weight on the driving wheels compared with the 4-6-0s.

What Bulleid really wanted to do was to make his mark by building a fleet of large express passenger engines, which would have elevated him to the status of Nigel Gresley on the LNER or William Stanier of the LMS, who were both household names and had been knighted. However, the Board of the Southern Railway was more concerned with electrification and wouldn't authorize the money, so Bulleid's first few years in office were spent tinkering about with existing designs and also with introducing new coaching stock. When the war came along and with it a massive increase in freight and troop train movements, there was a pressing need for more mixed traffic engines like the 'Black Fives' of the LMS, the 'Halls' on the Great Western or the similar-sized and often underrated 'B1s' of Edward Thompson on the LNER which was the latter's first design after inheriting Gresley's job. This was Bulleid's chance and the drawing office at Eastleigh was immediately kicked into life. What emerged however was not a simple mixed traffic 4-6-0 but the highly innovative three-cylinder 'Merchant Navy' class Pacifics. Anybody looking at these engines today, would say without hesitation that they were out and out express passenger engines, albeit with 6 ft 2 in. driving wheels instead of the more usual 6 ft 8 inch. I would have loved to be a fly on the wall at the meeting where he persuaded the Board that they were really suitable for mixed traffic; indeed, I certainly don't remember ever seeing one on a freight train in all my time as a trainspotter.

When the first locomotive appeared in 1941, it must have caused astonishment amongst the railway fraternity, for never before had so many new ideas been tried out all in one go. The fact that some of these innovations proved unreliable and were subsequently discarded, does not detract in any way from Bulleid's bold vision, which was to produce powerful locomotives that needed much less preparation by the driver and lower maintenance than conventional types and could therefore spend more time on the road and less in the shed. Initially at least, the engines must have been deemed a success, because after the 30 'Merchant Navy' class had been built, a further 110 of the slightly smaller 'West Country' and 'Battle of Britain' variety were sanctioned from 1945

Unrebuilt Bulleid Pacific No. 34007 *Wadebridge* about to depart from Alton.   *Author*

Another unrebuilt Bulleid Pacific. This time it is a visitor to the Mid Hants Railway: 'Battle of Britain' class No. 34081 *92 Squadron* in the original Southern Railway malachite green livery with yellow stripes.   *Tony Wood*

onwards. In appearance, these were virtually identical, the only difference being the firebox, which was about a foot shorter and the cylinders, which were reduced from 18 in. diameter down to just over 16 in. The boilers were rated at 250 psi instead of 280, which together with a few other minor changes saved around 8 tons in weight. The lower axle loading of these 'Light Pacifics' meant that they had a much greater route availability and they ranged over nearly all the Southern system.

Someone once said that the power of a steam locomotive depended upon its ability to boil water and although this is a rather simplistic view and does not take into account the effects of superheating and whether or not the valve gear is good enough to enable the steam to be used efficiently, it is basically correct. Bulleid took the argument a stage further by saying that the power of an engine depended upon its ability to burn coal - and if this is true, then he certainly succeeded with his Pacifics, which could gobble fuel at an alarming rate when working hard. Having said that, however, there is no doubt that the boilers were amongst the best steam raisers in the country.

With their all-welded construction, which itself was an innovation, they were cheaper to construct compared with the traditional flanged and riveted types that all the other companies were still using. The boiler pressure was originally set at 280 psi, which was the highest that had ever been used on a conventional locomotive in regular service - 220 to 250 being the usual range for express engines. It is possible that Bulleid may have been trying to ensure his new engines did not lose out in the tractive effort league table, which was featured prominently in the railway press before the war, for with this pressure the figure came out close to Gresley's 'A4s', although still quite a bit less than Stanier's Pacifics or the Great Western 'Kings'.

After the engines had been in service for a few years, it was found that the extra boiler pressure gave no real advantage and as the drivers could spin the wheels just as easily at 250 psi anyway, the boilers were all down-rated to this figure.

Another unusual feature of the boilers - at least in British practice, was the fitting of two thermic syphons in the firebox. These devices are rather difficult to describe but one could start off by imagining an ordinary tin funnel of the sort that might come in handy when filling your car petrol tank from a can. If you now flatten the large end down to about the same thickness as the spout, so that it has two 'Y' shaped parallel sides and finally bend the spout through some 60 degrees while keeping it in line with the flattened end, then you should have an idea of the shape. The syphons are welded in, with the small ends attached to the lower front face of the firebox and the longer upper ends going into slots cut into the crown sheet (the roof of the inner firebox). Syphons have the advantage that they provide valuable additional heating surface in the hottest part of the firebox and promote a vigorous circulation of the boiler water, which is drawn in at the lower ends and exits over the crown. Being flat, the upper sections have to be stayed against the internal water pressure in the same way as the firebox sides. In service, the syphons were relatively trouble free, apart from occasional cracking where they were welded into the firebox front plate and erosion on the elbow, where the section changed from flat to circular and which was constantly being bombarded by the coal being heaved in. They remained a feature of the engines right up to the end of steam on the Southern in 1967.

In appearance, the most visible departure from the conventional locomotive was the fitting of the slab sided boiler cladding or 'air smoothed casing' as Bulleid preferred it to be called. I read somewhere that the idea of this was that the locomotives could be cleaned by driving them through the carriage washing plants. Whether this was ever done or not I am unable to say, although I would imagine that it would have been pretty unpopular with the crews, who would have been unable to evade the torrent of water that entered the cab through the gap between engine and tender. As it was, the absence of the usual running plate above the wheels meant that the cleaners in the sheds had to be provided with ladders in order to clean the boiler sides. At the front, the chimney was recessed into the flat top of the casing, and this, coupled with the very soft exhaust beat from the multiple jet blast pipe, meant that the smoke was not lifted clear of the boiler and tended to drift back down the boiler sides and obscure the driver's vision - a fault I might add, that was not just confined to Bulleid's engines. Over the years, the quest for more powerful engines meant bigger boilers, and in order to remain within the loading gauge, bigger boilers meant shorter chimneys. Unless the engine was working hard enough to lift it, the problem of drifting smoke became a growing nuisance - Stanier's Pacifics, especially in their streamlined form, were especially prone to it. From the front, the casing had a roughly trapezoidal section, which was reminiscent of the shape of a well known brand of tinned meat and led to the locomotives being unkindly nicknamed 'Spam Cans' - a title they have been stuck with ever since.

Another departure from convention was the wheels, which instead of being spoked, were cast with alternate bosses, recesses and lightening holes. The idea had been tried in America but Bulleid's engines were the only ones to be fitted with them in this country. There was a small weight saving compared to normal spoked wheels and they were easier to clean - on the outside at any rate. The diameter was fixed at 6 ft 2 in. presumably to maintain the mixed traffic pretensions of the engines but to ensure that fast running was still possible, the stroke of the three cylinders was reduced to 24 in., which compared with 26 in. on Gresley's Pacifics and 28 in. on the Stanier variety. As with motor cars, a shorter stroke gives lower piston speeds, which reduces the out of balance forces and therefore permits higher revolutions per minute. The Southern did not possess any real racing grounds like Stoke bank on the LNER but even so, there have been numerous instances of these engines attaining over 100 mph in normal service.

If we take a look now at the footplate, there were still further novelties to be seen, including steam-operated firedoors, electric lighting and a steam reverser. The firedoors were in two semi-circular halves pivoted at the top and could be operated by the fireman using a foot pedal. This was ideal when it was necessary to open and shut the doors between each shovelful of coal to maintain the maximum heat in the firebox. There was of course a manual lever provided as well, if there was insufficient steam to work the device, or when the doors needed to be set partly open to control the smoke after firing a round. On

Swanage, which is the only Bulleid Pacific I have fired up to now, this particular gizmo has been removed, so I have never been able to find out what it feels like if your foot slips off the pedal when firing and the doors slam shut on the shovel!

The electric power was produced by a small steam driven turbo-generator beneath the footplate and provided enough electricity for the running lights as well as footplate and water gauge illumination. On the Mid-Hants, it has one other great benefit as well - if you are worried about blowing off steam in a station and have no water space left in the boiler to keep the engine quiet, the generator can always be run up, which given time will use up a bit of water.

On the driver's side of the cab, the most notable feature was the big space that existed where the lever or screw reversing gear would have been fitted on most other locomotives. Instead, there was just one small handle alongside the driver's seat. This had to be pushed forward or back to determine which way the gear would move, and was then lifted up to apply steam and set the cut-off and finally put down again to lock it. There was also a scale and pointer which was supposed to indicate the actual cut-off of the valve gear. Steam reversers on locomotives were not a new idea and several tried and tested designs were around if Bulleid had wanted one to copy, including one by Drummond, many of whose engines were still in service on the Southern at this time. Bulleid was his own man, however, and had one produced especially for his Pacifics and this, coupled with the unique chain driven valve gear, turned out to be the Achilles heel of the locomotives in their original form.

Unless fresh out of the works, the reverser appeared to have a mind of its own, and could creep into full gear and rarely, but even more dramatically, into back gear, when running ahead, without being touched by the driver! Small movements of the operating lever could cause large changes in cut-off, which meant that the drivers were discouraged from adjusting it to suit the gradients and instead, might only 'notch up' once after leaving a station and thereafter, adjust the power requirements with the regulator. This meant that the engines were usually being worked in longer cut-offs than similar-sized conventional locomotives and were very heavy on coal and water as a result. To compound the difficulties, the cut-off indicator, which was a rather delicate design and easily knocked out of adjustment, rarely told the truth, which meant that the only way the driver had of knowing how hard his engine was being worked, was to stick his head out the window and listen to the noise from the chimney! As I have explained before, the engines had a very soft exhaust beat, so the drivers could be easily be fooled into setting a longer cut-off than necessary. Peter Smith, who was an engineman on the old Somerset & Dorset route, recalls in his book, frequent occasions with these engines pulling heavy trains, when they were blasting away up the Mendip gradients with the pointer on the scale cheerfully indicating mid-gear and once or twice, even showing somewhere in back gear!

Turning now to the valve gear itself, upon which a great deal of abuse has been heaped in the past, we really need to take a look to see where Bulleid was coming from, rather than condemning the man without trial. Before Bulleid, all locomotives were lubricated on the 'total loss' system - the driver went round the engine and filled up all the oiling points at the start of his turn and during the course of the day's running it all leaked away onto the track or got plastered over the wheels and motion *en route*. Apart from the cost of the oil, it usually meant over an hour's work for the driver in the shed before the engine turned a wheel.

Where an engine had inside cylinders and motion, and in 1941 these were still in the majority, the driver had to crawl about inside the works with his oil feeders and flare lamp to complete the job - not a very pleasant start to the day's work even when the engine was over a pit - and also dangerous if any other engines were moving about. Over the years, a number of drivers were killed or seriously injured by being crushed in the motion when other engines accidentally buffered up and moved them. Now imagine the same job on a winter's day, with bitter cold, driving rain and no pit. The driver would be forced to crawl over the compacted wet and filthy ash that comprised the yard surface to get between the wheels to obtain access, his flare lamp would probably blow out and every time he heard an engine moving about the yard he would be worrying whether it might be the one that killed him. Small wonder then, that the drivers at least, were more than happy when Bulleid decided to encase all the inside motion in an oil bath, so they would never have to go under again. To oil up a Bulleid Pacific, all the driver had to do was take his feeder down the outsides to do the rods then fill up a couple of large oil trays on the footplate that fed the axlebox assemblies and finally, a mechanical lubricator which could be filled from the front apron below the smokebox door. Periodically, the fitting staff would check the oil level in the sump and top it up as required. Of course, Bulleid wasn't merely trying to be nice to the drivers, he believed that apart from the lower oil consumption, the maintenance costs would also be reduced; by keeping the valve gear totally enclosed and away from all the usual steam engine dirt and dust the engines therefore, as well as the footplate crews, would spend more time out on the road pulling trains - basically an admirable set of objectives.

In practice, it was found that it was impossible to keep the oil bath free from leaks due to the constant vibration, flexing of the frames and the driving axle jumping up and down on its springs, so that in many cases the engines finished up using more oil than before. I think that even using modern seals and gasket materials we would be hard put to effect a complete cure but until someone, in this case Bulleid, had the courage to try it out, the difficulties would never have been known. This oil continued to leak even when the engines were standing - notably at the ends of the platforms where the engines waited before leaving with their trains and some of it inevitably found its way onto the rails and caused slipping problems. At places like Waterloo station, the ballast was black with oil and slipping was so common that it became know as 'Spam start'. This reputation for slipping was, I believe, rather exaggerated and given a dry rail and a half-decent driver, the engines were little different from any other Pacifics, although they would get worse as the engines became more run down. One other unwelcome effect of this oil leakage, was that some of it was thrown off by the wheels and soaked into the lagging under the boiler, where it occasionally caught fire due to sparks thrown off by the brake blocks.

Conventional Walschaerts valve gear derives its motion jointly from the piston crossheads, which are connected to the valve spindles via the combination levers and by return cranks fitted to the driving axle crank pins, which operate the eccentric rods, these in turn operating the expansion links. With the valve gear for the outside cylinders now being moved in between the frames, an alternative means of driving it had to be found and Bulleid decided to use a separate valve crankshaft. This was chain driven from the driving axle and operated the combination levers and the eccentric rods for the three sets of valve gear. The drive was first taken across horizontally to a layshaft by one chain and then downwards to the crankshaft in the bottom of the sump by another, which allowed the driving axle to move vertically up and down on its springs without straining the valve crankshaft, which was fixed. To get all this lot into the oil bath meant that the gear had to be of a reduced size and the feature that struck me most when I first looked inside the works was how small the expansion links were - more the sort of size you would expect to find on a narrow gauge engine. The valve travel produced by this gear was of course also reduced in proportion and to obtain the desired stroke at the valve spindles, it had to be multiplied up by rocking levers adjacent to the valve chests in the ratio of 3 to 8.

One final departure from conventional practice, was that the piston valves were arranged for outside steam admission instead of inside. Piston valves consist of two valve heads on a spindle, spaced about two feet apart and working over the ports cut into the valve liners. The normal arrangement was for steam from the boiler to be introduced into the space between the valve heads and exhausted at the ends, so that the spindle glands were only subject to exhaust steam pressure and leakage would be kept to a minimum. On Bulleid's engines, the valve operating shafts entered the piston valve chests in this middle space and I surmise that Bulleid reasoned that this was going to be the most likely source of a leak - hence his decision for outside admission. In practice, the valve spindle glands, which were now subject to full boiler pressure, never gave very much trouble.

As I said in the introduction to this book, these engines are still subject to a great deal of controversy amongst steam buffs and now I get to the point where I attempt to explain the problems of the valve gear, one half of my readers will probably nod their heads in agreement with me, while the other half will say what a load of cobblers or something even less polite! I think it only fair to say, however, that from personal observation, the people I have met who are fans of these engines in their original form are, without exception, those who have never had to do any work inside the oil bath! Included in this category, of course, are quite a few of the drivers who, as I have explained before, were very happy to have an engine that did not require oiling underneath and which could pull any size train that the traffic department of the Southern cared to hang on the back of them. Critics included the shed fitters who had the unenviable task of repairing them, the shedmasters who frequently found themselves short of engines when they were stopped for maintenance or broken down and the firemen, who had to shovel a lot more coal than they did before. For myself, I have to say that I love any big steam engine and despite the heat and the hard work, I wouldn't have missed any of my firing turns on *Swanage* for anything.

I shall start this appraisal of the valve gear with the driving chains, which some critics have blamed for almost every defect of the engines. I once had a conversation with a former draughtsman from Eastleigh, where the engines were built, who said that Bulleid originally intended to use gear drive but as there is normally little requirement for gear cutting in a conventional locomotive, it meant that the job would have had to have been done by an outside factory. All these were fully occupied with war work making sprockets for tanks and the like, hence the decision to adopt chains instead. In service, the chains soon became worn and stretched, the effect of which, except in one special case which I will explain later, was to make the valve timing late - but that was all that it did. Walschaerts gear is normally arranged so that steam is admitted to the cylinders slightly before the piston reaches the end of its stroke - this is called lead (to rhyme with bleed) steam and is designed to improve fast running when the engine is on a short cut-off. The slack chains therefore, would give negative lead and a later cut-off. When you consider that nearly all Great Western two-cylinder engines were set with negative lead in full gear and were renowned for being amongst the quickest starting engines in the country, the reader might think that the late timing was no real disadvantage. However, the GWR engines employed a form of Stephenson's valve gear, where the lead increases as the cut-off is shortened and it is set so that it becomes positive again at the running cut-offs. With the Bulleid gear on the other hand, the engines are stuck with the late timing at all settings of the reverser.

There is actually an adjustment to take up slack in the chains but this means draining out the 40 gallons of oil and then releasing dozens of small bolts just to drop the lower cover plate to get at it - a detestable job, as I can vouch from personal experience and one which would mean the engine being out of service for a whole day. In any event, slack in the chains is only part of the problem and there would also be the wear in the numerous pins and bushes of the gear to deal with, especially at the 3 to 8 levers which weren't actually in the oil bath; unless these were overhauled at the same time, which would have stopped the engine for even longer, it would hardly have been worth doing.

The special case I mentioned, occurs when the locomotive has backed down onto its train and is coupled up. The reverser is now moved from reverse to forward gear, which resets the valves to the required positions (approximately) but the valve crankshaft will not move until the driving axle has rotated enough to take up all the slack. This means that just until the engine makes its first move, the late valve timing has now become early by the same amount. Any lost motion from the other components will add to this effect, so that with badly worn gear, the timing at this critical stage could be very early indeed, possibly with one piston taking steam on the wrong side whilst another has had it cut off when it should still be pushing. One can imagine the driver being given the 'right away' and attempting to get his temperamental charge to move off; first he gives a gentle pull on the regulator but nothing happens, a bit more and still nothing, finally, when there is nearly full boiler pressure in the steam chests, the one cylinder that is actually best placed for starting, defeats any adverse effects from the other two and the wheels start to move. Under these circumstances, a massive wheel slip is almost inevitable, due to the large volume of steam that has already got past the regulator. The snatch in the chains as they are suddenly brought up tight, is enough to make any engineer wince just thinking about it. The only other option available is to set back a few feet and try again with the wheels in a different position.

It is a rather strange fact that three-cylinder engines generally, are far more likely to suffer a refusal to start than two cylinder types - even when they don't have Bulleid valve gear! How can this happen? Three double acting cylinders will after all give six impulses for each turn of the wheel, instead of four, so they should be better at starting not worse. I was talking about this phenomenum recently to Frank Boait, our mechanical foreman, and he propounded the theory (and it is one which I fully endorse), that the extra cylinder simply means more places that the engine can be stopped 'wrong' for re-starting. Suppose that one cylinder is stopped on front or back dead centre and will therefore produce zero starting torque. The second cylinder will be 60 degrees past dead centre and will be well placed to push, but not at its maximum. The last cylinder will be 120 degrees past dead centre and will already be on the point of having the steam cut off by the valves; a fraction further and it will be exhausting anyway, so no help there. As the cylinders will be smaller than on similar-sized two-cylinder locomotives, the starting torque available will actually be quite a bit less at these six points than the worst case scenario for a two-cylinder engine (only four points). For comparison, 'Britannia' Pacifics had 20 in. cylinders with 28 in. stroke producing 32,150 pounds of tractive effort and were much better starters than 'Merchant Navies', which had 18 in. cylinders with 24 in. stroke and gave the slightly larger tractive effort of 33,495 pounds.

When considering the effects of wear in the linkages it has to be remembered that any error here will be multiplied up by the rocking levers in the ratio of 3 to 8, so to make an easy example, if the total free play in the valve gear was three eighths of an inch, by the time it got to the valve spindles it would have grown to a full inch. With a maximum design valve travel of around six and half inches, it can be seen that this would give a very significant loss of travel and hence a reduced cut-off available for starting - but only at low speeds. At higher engine speeds, the picture changes completely; the valves and valve rods together weigh several hundred pounds and once they get moving, they aquire momentum. Depending on several factors such as how hot they are, how tight the rings are in the valve liners and how much oil is around, there will come a point at which the momentum will overcome the friction and instead of stopping at the ends of their travel, when the valve gear stops pushing, they will carry on going until the lost motion is taken up - the valve travel has now been increased by the same amount that had been lost before. It is difficult to predict at what speed this phenomenum will occur, but my guess would be somewhere between 25 and 50 mph and of course, it will vary from one engine to another and even between individual cylinders on the same locomotive. This of course helps explain some of the extremely strange and uneven exhaust beats that often accompany the workings of an unrebuilt Bulleid Pacific!

I have read several performance logs of these engines where the recorder has noted something along these lines: 'A sluggish start was made from 'X' but by the time 'Y' was reached, the driver really opened up and a brilliant run was made as far as 'Z' which was reached on time, despite the slow start'. Did the driver really open up, or was it just a case of the valve gear starting to over-run and giving him perhaps an extra 10 per cent cut-off, without him adjusting the gear at all? I can recall quite clearly a run from Tonbridge to Ashford with one of these engines, which exactly mirrored the above circumstances. The start from Tonbridge was very slow and by Paddock Wood which is five miles out, the train was still doing barely 40 mph. By Marden though, it was up to 70 and by Headcorn to 90, with an arrival in Ashford around two minutes early. I can just imagine that fireman sitting on his seat taking it easy as the engine plodded off and then suddenly finding his fire disappearing up the chimney as fast as he could shovel it on - happy days!

The engines lasted in their original form until 1955, when their heavy coal consumption and maintenance costs had reached unacceptable proportions. The drawing office at Eastleigh decided that the only long term solution was a drastic rebuild and the scrapping of the controversial valve gear. This was a major task and involved casting a completely new inside cylinder block - this time with inside admission piston valves (the original outside admission cylinders were retained for the outside cylinders). Three sets of conventional Walschaerts valve gear were fitted, with the inside set being driven by an eccentric. The air-smoothed casing also disappeared and was replaced by normal cylindrical cladding. In appearance, the rebuilds still retained a certain individuality, with their strange wheels, large smoke deflectors and oval smokebox doors - to my mind every bit as impressive as their contemporaries on other lines and less dated.

The first of the rebuilt engines came into service the following year and soon showed themselves to be reliable and economical. The poor old drivers, of course, were now back underneath again with their oil feeders before every shift - this alone would be enough to account for any lack of enthusiasm on their part. Eventually all the 'Merchant Navies' and nearly half the 'Light Pacifics' were converted, before the demise of steam brought the programme to an end. Critics of the rebuilds usually say that in their new form the engines were boring and predictable and generally lacking the sparkle of the originals; none of these worthies, however, have been able to explain how it can be a disadvantage for the driver to be able to put the valve gear where he wanted it and for it to be doing what it was supposed to do. It is also a fact that during 1966 and 1967, which were the last years of steam on the Southern, there was more fast running over the West Of England main lines than at any time before - and nearly all of it was being done by the rebuilt variety.

Chapter Seven

A Firing Turn on *Swanage*

Having given the Bulleid controversy another good stir, I shall now give an account of what turned out to be one of my hardest days on the railway and which was also my final firing turn on *Swanage*, as the engine is now unfortunately out of service, collecting bird droppings and rust, as it awaits its turn for complete overhaul. This turn took place in early summer 1996 with Dave Wiseman junior as driver. The cleaner didn't turn up which suited me just fine, as I still had not got in many firing turns and felt the need to prove to myself I could fire a big engine all day on my own.

In retrospect this was rather optimistic seeing as I had only completed five firing turns prior to this.

Having signed on and read the notices, I strolled down to the engine, collecting some old rags from the shed *en route*. At this time of year, it was already broad daylight and promised to be a fine sunny day, which made preparation quite a pleasant job for a change. *Swanage* had about two inches of water in the glass and some 40 lb. of steam on the clock, so I could take my time with fire cleaning and ash disposal.

The lighting-up procedure for these Pacifics is no different from any other engine, except that it takes an awful lot more coal just to get the grate covered. Any really big lumps that came down to the shovelling plate as I coaled the box, were carefully swung into the back corners or under the door, while the smaller pieces got thrown over the middle and down the front. The usual stack of wood went in next, down under the brick arch, with some paraffin soaked rags in amongst it and to finish off, about another dozen shovels of coal were spread on top - perhaps half a ton of coal had gone in already but it still didn't look much in that cavernous firebox!

Lighting up a steam engine has for me a certain mystical quality; having done most of the dirty preparation work, there comes the moment when you light the magic match and bring the sleeping giant to life - except that on this occasion the matches were damp and wouldn't strike!

Feeling rather like Dr Frankenstein might have done after throwing the switch on his monster and finding there was a power cut, I wandered back to the shed in the hope of finding another box of matches on one of the workbenches. Having looked all over the place and drawn a blank, as a last resort I was reduced to striking sparks off the grinding wheel against a piece of scrap steel, in an attempt to set light to a piece of oily rag. This also appeared to be fire-proof and I was on the point of giving up, when a voice behind me suggested that I borrowed his lighter instead, as it was much easier that way! Turning round, I found one of the shed staff who had turned up early and having gratefully accepted his offer I was finally able to get *Swanage* alight.

With the blower cracked open just enough to send the smoke up the chimney instead of seeping out around the firedoors and covering everything in soot, I could sit down for five minutes and take a swill from my lemonade bottle

Bulleid 'West Country' class Pacific No. 34105 *Swanage* in original form and painted in BR livery running round the train at Alton. *P. Goodworth*

Bulleid 'West Country' class Pacific No. 34105 *Swanage* runs into Ropley with a train for Alton. *P. Goodworth*

before starting on the other chores - which included doing the driver's oiling as he hadn't yet turned up. I had finished doing the outside motion and was in the process of filling the large oil trays on the footplate when a friendly voice from below announced his arrival. After enquiring what exactly I had oiled, he took over where I left off and I decided that I might as well trim the tender now, while I was still dirty.

Until we had burned off a ton or two of coal, the doors into the bunker would remain closed, otherwise there would be a minor avalanche down onto the footplate and we could be knee deep in the stuff. On these engines, the gap between the cab roof and the tender front is very tight, so with the tender doors closed, I had to climb down from the cab and then back up the steps at the rear of the tender in order to reach the summit of the coal heap. *Swanage* has the earlier style tender, where the sides are raised level with the cab roof and continue right down to the rear. This leaves a convenient trough on either side of the coal bunker where the fire irons are stowed - and which also collects any coal which may have been spilled during the bunkering process. I picked up all these lumps by hand first and threw them inboard, then started shovelling and booting the main heap forward to fill the hole that had been created when I first coaled the firebox - the more I could get up front now, the further the engine would go before I had to repeat this tiring performance. I was pleased to find quite a few really decent lumps, about the size of a small kitchen pedal-bin, which were ideal to drop in the back corners of the firebox.

From my lofty perch I could see that the heavy smoke from the chimney had now reduced to a light brown, so it was time to put a bit more on the fire; I climbed down off the tender and then back up again to the footplate to spread a few shovels over the thin places and built up the back end a bit more. With the tender now levelled off and the fire made up, I made another trip to the shed and back to collect the lamps and discs, which meant more climbing about at the front and rear of the engine to reach the appropriate positions. Then it was back to the shed yet again for a can of water treatment and a final one-handed climb up the back of the tender to reach the tank lid - who needs aerobics in this game? This done, I retired to the 'Manor' for a brew and then got cleaned up and changed into my firing overalls - these had now been washed enough times to have changed their colour from navy blue down to a medium blue/grey colour - so I was at least beginning to look the part.

Back on board again feeling much refreshed, I found we had about 180 pounds on the clock with the fire burning nicely all over. This was enough pressure to test both injectors and I also took the opportunity to apply the 'pep pipe' and give the footplate a good wash down. While I played the boiling water around, visibility was virtually nil but as soon as I shut it off, it was quickly restored again, as the steam got sucked in through the open firedoors like water going down a plughole.

Having attended to the housework, there was still about 20 minutes before we were due off shed, which was just enough time for me to practise my culinary skills by cooking breakfast in the shovel. For those who might fondly imagine that bacon and eggs cooked in this way has some special flavour that is unobtainable by other methods, I can assure them that it is no different from that produced in a frying pan on your kitchen stove - except that the latter version will probably be lacking in all those little black specks that seem to get included, however much you clean the shovel first! I am not about to give a cookery lesson here but mention a few pointers that are worth considering.

First, choose your weapon: a Great Western shovel is ideal for those with very large appetites or when cooking for more than two persons, while the standard South African Railways shovel, which is in popular use on the Mid-Hants, comes a good second. For a normal crew of two, the ex-British Railways Lucas shovels as used on the Midland and Southern are the Rolls Royces in this field, being of heavy gauge steel which hold a good reserve of heat - even Delia Smith would approve. Mr Beesley's shovels, as supplied to the preservation movement today, are a little thin for cooking and need frequent insertions over the fire to maintain the heat, while the ex-LNER shovels, which were designed to go through the half moon openings in their firedoors, are really a bit on the small side.

When cooking, it is usually only necessary to poke the shovel over the fire for a few seconds at a time to maintain the temperature - in fact, if you keep it in too long and allow the hot fat to run down over the end of the blade, the whole lot may burst into flame! It also most inadvisable to have the shovel in when the engine is about to move off - the first exhaust beat will suck your breakfast straight off the shovel, through the tubes and send it up into space!

Having eaten our egg and bacon rolls and also supplied one for Dave Sibley, who seemed to have the uncanny knack of being able to sniff out a fry-up even from inside the shed, it was time to move off down to Alresford to pick up our train. With nothing to do for now, I could sit on my seat and relax with another lid of tea while Dave watched the road. The footplate was already hot enough for him to have removed his jacket, but I kept mine on - when firing to the back corners, the leading hand finishes each swing right up in the mouth of the firehole and even though it is only there for a split second, a bare arm can still get scorched without protection.

In Alresford we found our train waiting as usual in the up platform - there were six coaches on this occasion. We were informed that there was no shunter available, so this meant that I would have to hook on and off at each end of the line - an additional chore I could well have done without. There was a good crowd of passengers on the platform, some of whom observed me wrestling with the brake hoses as I coupled up, but at least there would be no need to connect the steam heating pipes as well on such a hot day. Climbing back onto the platform, I walked down to the station buffet and collected another couple of drinks for Dave and myself, before returning to the engine.

With 15 minutes to go before departure, I picked up the shovel and started building up my fire, shovelling solidly and fast for the next 10 minutes, which was enough to bring the back of the fire up to within six inches or so below the firehole - and also to start the perspiration dripping off my face. A brief pause to snatch another few mouthfuls of tea, then I bent my back once more and heaved about 15 shots down each side. This left a horseshoe-shaped fire, thick at the back and down the sides but very thin in the middle and across the front.

When we got the 'right away', I partly closed the firedoors and then watched the train out of the platform. Dave started *Swanage* away without slipping and we accelerated smoothly under Sun Lane bridge before he started to 'notch up' the valve gear. This he did with short up and down movements of the lever - really hardly more than flicks of the wrist. It seemed rather incongruous that such delicate movements could control this great fire breathing monster and it looked pretty tricky to hit the right spot.

Dave explained that a simple modification had been carried out on the reversing cylinder to make it less sensitive and easier to set, this being to replace the water that originally filled it with heavy steam oil. The vastly increased viscosity of the oil has the effect of slowing down the movement of the gear; before this had been done it must have been terribly easy to overshoot the desired position.

Having started with such a big fire, all I needed to do on this short leg was splash about eight shovels across the thin places at the front of the grate, while the heaped-up coal at the back was pulled down by the blast and fed the middle. We rolled into Ropley in fine style with around 240 psi on the clock and three-quarters of a glass of water. I whacked another dozen into each back corner as we stood in the station and soon it was time to go again.

This coal had a lot of volatile matter and the firedoor stayed partly open the whole time to control the smoke and allow the gases to burn off. *Swanage* was steaming superbly and we stormed away up the 1 in 60 as if it was on the level, with an air of confidence prevailing on the footplate. I started firing again, six at a time, mostly down the sides and just inside the doors, where the fierce blast took it straight down the slope. I tried to throw a few more into the back corners, but the strength of the draft through the firehole sucked on the blade of the shovel as I turned it sideways to get round the corner and tried to drag it forward, so I wasn't sure where it finished up - not that it seemed to matter very much, as the pressure gauge was still right on the red line. In fact, I was a bit slow getting on the injector and the safety valves lifted, which earned me a black mark - not the only one that day unfortunately. It was obvious we were not going to need any more coal on this leg so I took the opportunity to stick my head out into the breeze and cool off a bit, as the day was turning into a real scorcher.

Coming back from Alton we were delayed a few minutes while we waited for a family with a pushchair and a couple of toddlers in tow, to cross the footbridge from the BR station and descend the steps to our platform to catch the train. I looked at my watch and then at Dave who nodded in response to my unspoken query. We were both thinking the same thing: three minutes lost was to three to gain, so it looked as if he was going to have a real bash at the hill - I picked up the shovel and quickly slung on a few more lumps into the back corners.

Eventually our tardy punters were safely aboard and we received the whistle and green flag from the guard. *Swanage* hooted in reply and Dave gave the regulator a solid pull open and then immediately closed it again - nothing happened. Another pull open and push closed but this time there was movement and a muffled 'shoof' sounded from the chimney. Almost imperceptibly, we started to creep forward and Dave gave the cylinders more rapid shots of steam; further 'shoofs' followed and finally the regulator could be left partly open, while we negotiated the pointwork at the end of the platform and snaked out onto the running line.

No sand had been used and there had been no slipping - indeed, Dave performed this tricky feat some 20 odd times during the day, with barely a hint of 'Spam start' - I have seen Bulleid Pacifics slip on many occasions, even when 'light engine', so this was a quite an achievement.

When the last coach cleared the points, Dave heaved the regulator wide open and we started to accelerate rapidly. As the fire started to burn through, my boiler pressure began to rise, so it was quickly on with the injector to avoid another blow off. By the time we crossed Butts bridge, we were doing 35 mph and *Swanage* had the bit between her teeth. The beautiful Hampshire countryside was rushing past but I had no time to admire the view; that ravenous furnace was now blinding white and I was having to stoke like a madman. The pressure was holding at about 240, with the water level bobbing at the top of the glass and we continued to gain speed, even up the 1 in 60.

I have had trips before and since this one, which have gone so well that I wished the hill could have been a bit longer - but this was not one of them; the heat and the exertion had taken their toll and I was more than happy when Dave gave me the crossed arm gesture to let me know I could pack up firing. I gratefully dropped the shovel in the coal hole and leant out the window to gulp down some cool air.

We were now approaching Hampshire Hunt bridge, which is just before Medstead distant signal and I wound the damper closed and put on the second injector; holding up two fingers to Dave to let him know I had done so. A few hundred yards past the distant and then he shut off steam - our momentum would easily carry us over the top from there. As the home signals came into view, they were all 'on' and we were brought to a stand while we waited for the up train to arrive. By the time a tired-looking 'S15' plodded into the platform and the signals cleared for us to run into the loop, we were still three minutes late, so all our time recovery efforts had been in vain - it was good fun trying though!

Having done my bit I could take it easy for the next six miles, while we rumbled down through Ropley and into Alresford once again. The good news here was that the traffic department had found a shunter for us, so I wouldn't have to do any more hooking on and off. The bad news, was that I had now used up all the readily available sizeable lumps and found that underneath there was a thick layer of small coal and dust, with most of it no bigger than a tennis ball. It was also wet and compacted from the pep pipe and refused to trim down on its own. Now small coal is fine once you are moving and have a decent bed of fire established, but to get that decent bed, you need lumps of a size that will not fall through the gaps between the firebars and which will allow the air to get up between them, so from now on, each trip was prefaced by a foray into the tender, to sling down some decent stuff to the shovelling plate. I had to admit to feeling a bit brassed off that it was necessary to start this unwelcome chore so early in the day but there it was, like it or not.

After I had thrown and shovelled down what looked like a decent pile, I wriggled over the top and back down to the footplate to start stuffing the firebox again. Despite the huge fire I started with from Alton and all that was shovelled on the way up the hill, the back end had dropped right down again and I could even see the firebars in one or two places further forward, so another massive coal heaving operation was required.

By now, the cab felt like an inferno, with the temperature up around 130, and each spell on the shovel had me breathing hard and dripping with sweat. We had the usual requests from the passengers to come up on the footplate; some got straight back off again; none stayed very long. As the last punter got down, Dave reappeared with a welcome tumbler of orange squash and an additional bottle already made up, which the catering crew had thoughtfully been keeping in the fridge for us. I slumped down in my seat and greedily guzzled my drink down all in one go, while Dave kindly picked up the shovel and put the finishing touches to the fire. When he had finished, that pile of lumps I had just thrown down were nearly all gone - and we hadn't even moved yet!

When we got away this time, I didn't bother to fire at all on the way to Ropley, because I knew we would be stopping there for water and it was best not to arrive with a big fire. The tender on *Swanage* holds 5,500 gallons of water and as were using a shade over 1,500 gallons each trip, it meant that we would need a water stop at some time during the day to top it up. It also meant that over the four round trips, my fire would have to convert some 6,000 gallons (that is about 27 tons!) of cold water, into steam at around 240 psi - no wonder we were gobbling coal so fast.

Dave stopped us just right for the column and I climbed down off the engine and picked my way over the point rodding to reach the back of the tender. Having climbed back up again to reach the tank lid, Dave threw me a rope and I pulled over the heavy swinging arm and poked the large diameter filling hose (for some reason always called the bag) into the tank. Dave opened the handwheel and water began to flood in. The force of the water tried to make the bag jump out again and I had to brace one knee against it to keep it down the hole. It was also spraying several fine jets of water out from various leaks and I bent my head under one and let the cold water run over my face and neck - heavenly.

Within a few minutes we had taken on some 3,000 gallons of water, which had got the tank nicely filled again and Dave wound the valve closed. The swinging arm of the column has a return arrangement to swing it back away from the track. This works on the same principle as a 'rising butt' door hinge but Dave secured it with the rope anyway - accidents have been caused in the past when a very high wind has blown one of these arms into the path of a passing train. Back on the engine, feeling at least temporarily refreshed after my impromptu cold shower, there was just time to bang yet another dozen shots into the back corners before we got the tip from the guard and were off once again.

The remainder of this trip and the next one passed without incident, except that I was finding the heat and the workload about as much as I could stand. Dave obviously sensed that I was flagging a bit and pulled the coal down for me at the Alton end, which was a great help. He also nipped into the buffet car at each end of the line to keep me provided with cold drinks, while I was bending my back and re-stuffing the firebox.

Tea would probably be more refreshing but there would not be enough time in a turn round to wait for it to cool down and drink it. The only way to keep going under these conditions is to keep on pouring down plenty of fluids and take salt - my own preferred snack is liberally salted tomatoes, which are a lot easier to swallow than crisps when your mouth is dry.

I know there are good reasons for normal people doing normal jobs to avoid taking too much salt - but this is not a normal job. When you are perspiring on this sort of scale, your body can become salt deficient very quickly, leading to exhaustion, cramps and finally a collapse with heat stroke - I have seen this happen several times on board ships in the tropics, invariably where the person concerned was not taking the standard issue salt tablets.

Back at Alresford we were preparing for our fourth and final round trip, where the effort of bringing the coal down and refilling the firebox just about finished me off. I was now wishing fervently that I hadn't been so cocky as to think I could handle this sort of job on my own. The back end of that firebox seemed like a bottomless pit and however much I shovelled into it, there was always room for more and the more I shovelled in, the further I had to reach back into the tender to get it. How in heavens name did those real firemen in steam days manage to put up with hard graft like this every time they went to work?

When one is hot and tired, it is easy to make a mistake and now I made one. Dave was off the engine and had asked me wait for a signal from the guard, before opening the cylinder cocks and putting on the small ejector to create the brake - (steam tends to build up in the cylinders when the engine is standing, due to leakage past the regulator and from the steam atomisers of the lubricators, so the cocks are opened to release any residual pressure, which could cause the engine to try and move once the brakes come off). I had forgotten all about this instruction until the signalman appeared with the token. With departure imminent, I assumed I must have missed the signal from the guard and duly opened the cocks and blew up the brake. Unfortunately, the shunter was still standing by the front of the engine when the blast of steam emerged from the pipes. This could have scalded him quite badly but mercifully did not and he soon appeared on the footplate to tell me what he thought of me - in language far more polite than I deserved, I might add.

Apart from being pretty well done in, I was also furious with myself over this incident, so by the time we reached Alton and I climbed into the tender for the last time to bring down the few remaining decent lumps of coal, I was feeling very despondent. While up in the tender I spotted a small boy, perhaps 8 years old on the platform with his Mum, looking excitedly up at the engine. I was not really in the mood to entertain visitors but there was something about the lad which stuck a chord - wasn't he a bit like me all those years ago, when I used to stand in smoky stations wishing I was an engine driver? I asked him if he wanted to come aboard and have a look round and he was up the cab steps like a shot.

When he had finished saying 'Cor' and 'Wow' I offered him the shovel and helped him put a bit of coal on. He was obviously thrilled to bits and didn't seem in any hurry to get off, despite the heat. Somehow, his enthusiasm rekindled my own and I determined that this last run would be a good one. Dave came back with an ice cream and finished building the fire so I had time to eat it. When it was time to go, the little boy climbed down, his Mum was full of smiles and I was feeling better.

After Dave's usual steady start, I picked up the shovel for the last bout of firing and got stuck in. All we had left now in the way of fuel was small coal and dust, which disappeared in a white flash the instant it hit the fire, producing one brief puff of brown smoke at the chimney for each shovel full. I read somewhere that feeding small coal to a Pacific working hard, is like feeding strawberries to a donkey - well, it isn't a bit like that. Donkeys are nice friendly animals and would be equally happy with a carrot, or even just a pat on the nose. They are not snatching their food as fast as you can throw it and roasting the chef at the same time! Despite this, I was still managing to keep the pressure up and it felt good to finish the day as well as we had started.

After we dropped off our train at Alresford, all that remained was to run light engine back to Ropley and put *Swanage* to bed. When I had opened the smokebox door, which is recessed back between the sides and top of the casing, I found the sulphurous fumes almost overpowering in the confined space. This made a rotten job even worse and I had to keep taking a step back, to get a breath of fresh air before diving in with the broom and shovel again. I was so tired that anybody watching me perform could be forgiven for thinking I was about 90 years old, judging by the speed I was going at, but eventually the job was done and we could retire to the 'Manor' for a pot of tea.

Dave is one of those drivers who is slow to chide and quick to praise, and he thanked me for a good day out and didn't mention the incident with the cylinder cocks. Although still very cross with myself, I had to confess to a certain amount of pride as well - Bulleid tenders hold about six tons of coal, and with a little help from my driver, I had pretty well emptied it, kept the pressure right up on all the climbs and the safeties had only blown off once.

As I said earlier *Swanage* is now cold and dead in the part completed running shed, waiting her turn in the repair queue, so I have no idea if and when I shall get another chance to fire her. *Bodmin* on the other hand, was beginning to look like a locomotive again, after years of being a pile of bits in the workshop and it would be interesting to see for myself how a 'rebuild' compared with the original type. It was also rumoured that we would have 'Merchant Navy' No. 35005 *Canadian Pacific* visiting the railway soon, which would give me an even bigger firebox to slave in front of - believe it or not, I was looking forward to it!

Three Pacifics at Ropley. Rebuilt 'West Country' No. 34016 *Bodmin* runs in past Nos. 60009 and 34081 in Ropley yard. *B. Zehetmayr*

Ropley yard at lighting up time - Nos. 34016 and 73096 on pit road with Nos. 41312, 92212 and 'Thomas' behind. The wheeldrop shed still minus the roof is clearly visible. *Gwen Cartwright*

Chapter Eight

Motive Power Miscellany

I have taken the title of this chapter from a regular feature that used to appear in *Trains Illustrated* magazine (and may still do so for all I know). This discussed the various locomotives that could be seen up and down the country and what they were doing there. *Trains Illustrated* incidentally, which appeared monthly, was my preferred reading matter, at a time when most of my contemporaries were reading about 'Roy of the Rovers' in their comics. Back in those days none of my class mates found this to be particularly unusual, which shows how times have changed - any child reading about trains in school today is liable to be teased and possibly even bullied, just for being a little different.

There was another regular column in the magazine, which listed engines that had been withdrawn from service and were destined for the scrapyard. By 1962 this had become a very long list indeed and when I started putting names to some of the numbers, I eventually found this obituary column too depressing to read and I ceased to be a subscriber - how on earth anyone could nonchalantly light a gas torch and cut up a 'Castle' or an 'A4', I cannot imagine. On the whole, I think the engines of the LNER had the most interesting and varied collection of names, with a lot of them being named after race horses, but there were also birds, characters from Sir Walter Scott's novels and of course that one very famous duck! I still feel quite sad even today, when I turn the pages of my Ian Allan book - it is like reading the names on a memorial tablet to the victims of some long forgotten tragedy: *Silver Link, Merlin, Golden Fleece, Hyperion, The White Knight, Grand Parade, Flying Fox, Redgauntlet, Saint Mungo, Steady Aim, Pearl Diver*, the nameplates on some collector's wall are all that remain.

I find it amazing that apart from Dai Woodham in Barry, none of the other big scrap dealers, or even British Railways themselves for that matter, ever had the foresight to leave one or two engines under a tarpaulin at the back of their yards and just forget about them for a few years. By 1980, when the preservation movement had really started to get going, even the rusting, cannibalised wrecks at Barry were being sold at many times their original scrap value. Imagine how much an 'A1' Pacific such as No. 60156 *Great Central* would be worth if it suddenly turned up on the market, rusting but complete? In restored condition today you would probably have to pay half a million pounds for a locomotive like this.

'A3' Pacific *Flying Scotsman* is probably the most famous steam engine in the world and is universally admired wherever it goes. Many people, however, are quite surprised to learn that there were originally another 77 engines just like it and that they all got scrapped. Whole classes of engine were systematically wiped out and to show just how great the slaughter really was. I give the following few examples: GWR 'Grange' and 'County' 4-6-0s and '4700' class 2-8-0s, none saved from 119; Southern 'King Arthur', 4-6-0, one left out of 54; LMS 'Patriot' 4-6-0, none saved from 52; LNER 'A1' 4-6-2, none saved from 50 (although there is a well-advanced project to build one from scratch!); LNER

'A2' 4-6-2, one left out of 40; LNER 'B1' 4-6-0, one saved from 409!; LNER 'B2' and 'B17' 4-6-0s, none saved from 59; LNER 'V2' 4-6-2, one saved from 184 - and these were just the more well-known types. Smaller engines such as 4-4-0s, which had been the mainstay of passenger services before the bigger ones came along, faired even worse; apart from a handful which had been taken by museums, such as the Great Western's *City of Truro*, scores of classes and thousands of engines disappeared without trace.

I knew in my heart of hearts that the change from steam to diesel and electric had to come; steam engines after all are very labour intensive, with poor availability and a very low thermal efficiency compared with more modern motive power - it was just the indecent haste of it all that I found so distressing. At a time of high unemployment when coal was cheap and oil was expensive, it would have made sound economic sense to carry on with the more modern steam engines for a few years longer. For example, many of the BR Standard engines had only just been built (*Evening Star* a class '9F' 2-10-0, which was the very last one, was completed in 1960!) and would have had many years useful life in them before needing major repairs - why not at least have got some return on the investment before scrapping them?

Fortunately, some engines did escape the scrapman's evil clutches and found their way into preservation, one of them being No. 30506, our 'S15' class 4-6-0. This particular engine is one of a family of similar types, which originated from a design by Robert Urie in 1915, these being the 'H15' class, which had 6 ft driving wheels and the more famous 'N15' or 'King Arthur' class with 6 ft 7 in. wheels. The 'S15' version was really designed as a goods engine and had 5 ft 6 in. wheels, although its long boiler with smoke deflectors and the impressive eight-wheel tender give it a more dashing appearance than most other freight designs. The cab, however, which has no side windows and a general lack of creature comforts on the footplate, mark the engine firmly down in the World War I period; when men were dying in their thousands in the mud of the Western front, minor details such as these were not considered worthy of consideration. The controls are much the same as on any other steam engine, with nothing very remarkable apart from the injector steam valves; for some strange reason these open clockwise, which is the opposite to just about any other valve I have ever come across and which invariably catch a new fireman out a few times before he gets used to them. Ergonomics were obviously not considered for the regulator either - this opens away from the driver and needs both hands when going onto second valve; as it cannot be operated whilst looking out of the cab at the same time, it makes buffering up onto the train quite a tricky job.

Out of all the engines I have fired on the Mid-Hants, No. 30506 has caused me more problems than the rest put together - either I've had so much steam I didn't know what to do with it or (more frequently), I've had to struggle for every pound I could get. Why this should be, I have no idea, although recently the engine has had its share of problems such as leaking tubes and heavy knocking in the axleboxes, which certainly haven't helped. Eventually the engine became so rough that it was withdrawn from service for a pretty major overhaul, with the boiler being removed from the frames for repairs, while the offending axleboxes were re-metalled and machined.

One of the worst days I have ever had (from the steaming point of view) took place immediately before this overhaul, when the engine really was on its last legs. The driver on this occasion was Dave Wiseman senior - the father of Dave junior from the previous chapter and again we had no cleaner.

Reading the notices, which mentioned various leaks in the firebox and the heavy knocking gave me a foretaste of what to expect - I was hardly surprised, therefore, when I first climbed up on the engine, to find there was no water in the gauge glasses and no steam on the clock either, so it already looked as if we might be in for a rough day. The first job, was to connect a hose to one of the injector overflow pipes and get some water back in the boiler. This took nearly 10 minutes before the level came back into sight and I carried on a bit longer to give myself a third of a glass, before I set about cleaning the grate and lighting the fire. Even with steam raised, there was still a very noticeable leak from somewhere down the right-hand front corner of the firebox and in fact, the fire never really got going in this area all day.

When we went off shed the sun was shining, which was just as well because we had no storm sheet and standing at Alresford before the first departure, with a fresh cup of tea in hand, it was very pleasant. I made up the fire as per usual and at the 'right away' we had nearly a full head of steam and three-quarters of a glass of water - all fine and dandy one might think. As soon as we got moving, the pressure began to drop but this was quite normal and I expected it to recover as the fire burned through and became really hot. Waiting for the smoke to clear, I fired three down the sides and two down the middle and then stood back and waited for the needle on the pressure gauge to start climbing again - unfortunately it carried on going down! Perhaps the fire was still a bit thin down the front end, so I quickly banged another four down in that direction and awaited results. There was a healthy amount of smoke but the pressure still just sat there and refused to climb. Eventually, I was forced to put the injector on as well, which sent the needle even further in the wrong direction. As we rolled into Ropley we were 40 lb. down and I had a good look at the fire to see what could be amiss. Apart from a black area where the water was leaking down in the front right corner, the firebed looked bright and even all over.

Now it is one thing to be short of steam and know the reason why, but it is even more worrying when you can't see anything wrong. Dave, however, didn't seem to be concerned at all and just left me to get on with it - unlike some drivers I could name, who would already be peering at the fire and telling you how to do the job. I set about recovering the pressure as quickly as I could - another dozen shovels mostly round the back end, close the doors, open the damper and screw the blower open wide. This gave me nearly the full 200 psi again by the time we left, but only half a glass of water. On the run up to Medstead I fired as carefully as I knew how - only three or four at a time and watching the smoke like a hawk to decide when to fire next. The engine responded rather better to this treatment but it was still a losing battle - either I could hold the steam at the expense of the water level, or maintain the water and lose the steam. As we were chimney first, I opted to sacrifice the steam to ensure there would be sufficient water when we nose-dived over the summit at Medstead, so the pressure was down to 150 psi by the time we reached the station.

After this dismal performance, I was determined to have a better start for the return trip and I started making up the fire again as soon as we arrived down in Alton. This time I built a really big one - right up to the firehole ring and then level for a couple of feet before tapering down to the front. I also took the time to nip down to the front end to recheck the smokebox door lugs - if the door is not firmly closed it can draw in air which will adversely affect the draught on the fire. Unfortunately however, I found they were all tight, so I was still none the wiser about the poor steaming. With a minute to go before departure, the fire was already burning through and I had a full glass with the pressure coming up to the mark. At this point, damn and blast it, the safeties decided to blow - still five pounds short of the red line. By the time they seated down again, we had lost another 10 pounds and there was no time to recover it because we had the 'right away' and Dave was whistling to go.

With the big fire I had on there was no need to add any more for the first half-mile and the pressure even began to rise slightly, but as soon as the injector went on, the needle once again began to crawl backwards down the scale. Dave was nursing the engine as much as he could, but all my best efforts on the shovel failed to prevent the decline and as we shut off for the summit there was a meagre 130 lb. pressure with the water barely visible in the bottom of the glass. The only thing that saved our bacon is that we were tender first and would regain at least half a glass of water as we went over the top. I was feeling both mystified and depressed at my lack of success but Dave was quite unperturbed. All he said was, 'We got here didn't we and with a quick turn round down the other end we shall even be back on time again, so why worry?' No criticism, no attempts to tell me what I was doing wrong - you would think that we had just run a normal trip!

It would be nice to report that things improved after this, but I am afraid that the pattern was set. I tried thick fires, thin fires, trough-shaped fires and 'haycock' fires in Great Western-style, but nothing really worked. In fact, the best I ever did before shutting off for the summit in the down direction was 140 psi and about an inch of water. As if this wasn't enough, on the final run, we ran into the mother and father of a thunderstorm coming down from Medstead and got soaked to the skin. As we rumbled into Alresford station for the last time, and disposed of our train, I muttered something about coming to the end of a perfect day and we both burst out laughing.

It was something of a relief to learn that everyone on the railway was now struggling for steam and one or two had even stalled on the bank, so it wasn't anything to do with my firing technique. The problem turned out to be the coal. The Railway has obtained its supply from a number of different sources over the years and this lot just happened to be a particularly bad batch - so much so, that we started calling it 'safety coal' because of its' reluctance to burn!

Dear Dave, apart from being an excellent engineman, he was one of the nicest men you could ever wish to meet. I am very sorry to say that he died on New Year's Eve 1999, a victim of the 'flu' epidemic then sweeping the country. He will be sorely missed by all who knew him on the Mid-Hants.

The trouble with writing a book like this, is that unless you wait until you retire before starting, events will continue to unfold as you write it and if you wish to include these in the narrative, then the chronology is bound to become somewhat disjointed - I had intended to leave No. 30506 at this point and move on to another engine but a couple of runs from May and June 2000 are worth including, both on Real Ale special trains.

These trains are run in the evenings after the regular service has finished and consist of two round trips over the line, during which the passengers may sample the pleasures of a ride behind a steam locomotive, whilst slaking their thirst with the aforesaid Real Ale in the well-stocked bar. The usual form is for the crew working the special to take over the engine at Ropley and run the stock down to Alton, where the train stands for an hour or so until the first departure which is at around 7 pm. One of the disadvantages of these turns, is that the engine will already have been in steam all day and may have a dirty fire, which will have to be cleaned before proceeding. The coal will also be well back in the tender and will usually be down to the smaller lumps and slack that could have been laying there undisturbed for a week or two. Other than that, it is quite pleasant to start one's turn in the afternoon for a change, with no crack of dawn start and all the dirty preparation work to do.

When the train rumbled into Ropley and stopped at the water column, my driver and I climbed aboard to take over. The crew we were relieving gave us the unwelcome news that the engine was not steaming very well and said they didn't think the coal was up to much. Having topped up the tender with water, I dropped down onto the footplate and we were soon on our way to Alton. It rapidly became apparent that the engine was not doing too well and it needed all my best efforts on the shovel to get us up to Medstead, by which time we had lost around 50 lb. of boiler pressure. Bob Cartwright, who was now my regular driver, didn't seem too worried, however, and said that we would have plenty of time to clean the fire down at Alton, which should put things somewhere near to rights.

We duly cleaned the fire as best we could but in the absence of a decent clinker shovel, had to content ourselves with simply breaking up whatever lumps we couldn't get out, which wasn't as good a job as we would have liked. Just in case the ashpan was blocked, which would also have an adverse effect on the steaming, I managed to wriggle about under the engine with the rake and did a half-decent job of emptying that as well, so we had done all we could under the circumstances.

About 25 minutes before departure I started to build up the fire, which had now actually gone out at the front end after all the poking and prodding. A few shovels spread over the remaining live fire were rapidly ignited, however, and were then pushed around with the long pricker to cover the dead areas. This treatment soon had things looking healthier, after which I constructed the usual wedge shaped fire - up to the firedoor at the back end and tapering down to one lump thick at the front.

At the 'right away' we had nearly a full glass and a full head of steam, leading me to announce to Bob that I had every confidence - which just goes to show how wrong you could be, even after doing the job for five years! Initially, things didn't look too bad and the boiler pressure actually began to rise very slightly, but this didn't last very long and as soon as the injector went on, the pressure gauge started sliding back the wrong way.

With a six-coach load on gradients like ours, the poor old 'S15' has to be really thumped to time a train; there can be no pussy footing around on first valve of the regulator or the train will simply stop, so second valve and around 40 per cent cut-off were the order of the day. As we passed Butts and got onto the steep part of the bank, the situation on the footplate was already looking grim, with the pressure down to about 170, by which time I had noticed that my big heap at the back of the box hadn't really got going and was still looking black! There is no point in ladling more coal onto a black fire, so it was down with the pricker instead, to try and get some air into that mass. This must have been at least partially successful because we were rewarded with a bit of welcome smoke from the chimney but the overall trend remained steadily down the nick. Between us we alternated between shovel and pricker and generally tried every trick we could think of just to keep going, but it was obvious that the fire was simply not getting enough air. By the time we reached Medstead distant we had only 120 pounds of steam with the water down to about an inch. I was convinced we would have to stop for a 'blow up' and I know some drivers who definitely would have, but Bob had done this job for real in BR days when he was a fireman at Eastleigh shed and knew to a fraction how far he could let it go. As 'Thank Christ' bridge appeared, the water had virtually disappeared, while the speed was down to about 10 mph, but by then the regulator could be eased back and the resulting slight deceleration was enough to bring a surge bobbing back into sight at the bottom of the glass. The feeling of relief was so great I yelled out to Bob 'I can see it' as if I had been Livingstone discovering the source of the Nile! A few more beats at the chimney took us over the top and the regulator could be shut, at which point the water came permanently back into view - it had been a close run thing.

It was obvious by now that something was seriously amiss with our reluctant steed and unfortunately we didn't know what! Even going down the hill with the firedoor shut and the blower screwed out, the boiler was pretty slow to recover and I began to have serious doubts that we would ever get back again. Bob, however, appeared to be relishing the challenge and reckoned that with a quick turn round we could recover some of our lost time and still make a go of it. Unfortunately, it wasn't just the engine having an off day, for after we had unhooked at Alresford and gone forward to run-round the train, the signalman gave us the dummy without first changing the points, so when Bob opened the regulator we went straight back the way we had come! Luckily we both spotted the error and my yell of 'Wrong road' to Bob coincided with him dropping the brake handle and we stopped long before there was any danger of hitting the train, but with the engine halfway across the offending points. Some of our passengers, who were by now fairly well lubricated and merry had gone up onto the footbridge to watch the manoeuvre and gave us a few ribald jeers for our pains, which did nothing for our self esteem. By the time Bob had got down to phone the signalman and we had duly repeated the shunt and coupled up again, we were nearly as late as we had been on arrival.

Somehow we managed to keep going and the second climb from Alton turned out to be slightly better than the first, which was quite an achievement under the circumstances, but by this time the train was running so late that there was a danger we would miss the connection with the last main line service out of

Alton. This would have left our passengers stranded, so we reluctantly had to call for assistance in the shape of a class '27' diesel from Ropley which took over our train, while we retreated ignominiously light engine back to the shed.

Bob Cartwright however, never uttered a word of complaint about the lack of steam which I had provided for him and it even became the start of a little joke between us. From now on we were never short of steam, we were merely practising 'negative boiler control', meaning there was no smoke, no steam, no water and no blowing off at the safety valves! Another standing joke originated from an occasion when I had been a bit slow opening the firedoors and applying the blower when Bob shut off, which resulted in an enormous pall of smoke issuing from the chimney. Knowing of my Marine background, he suggested that I might have been practising a re-run of the Battle of Jutland in 1915, when both the English and German navies laid smokescreens to put off the other side's aim!

Joking aside, this had been the most humiliating turn I had ever had on the Railway and when I found myself marked down again for the same job two weeks later and with the same engine, I was not looking forward to it one little bit. Meeting my driver (Bob again) in the shed beforehand though, he told me that following our little debacle, Bob Deeth had gone out on the engine and even he couldn't make it steam, which made me feel somewhat better. After this, the locomotive was withdrawn for a thorough investigation, which disclosed that the blast pipe was loose and had been drawing in air from the base of the smokebox, which meant we had been on a loser right from the start.

Having arrived with half an hour or so to spare, Bob and I occupied ourselves with an old clinker shovel which we found lying in the yard. It was badly beaten about and distorted but we took it into the workshop and managed to hammer it back into some sort of shape, so we would be better prepared if we needed to clean the fire again. Then we strolled over to the bank by the water column to await the train. Bob enjoined me to take care when walking through the weedy undergrowth on the chalky bank as adders have quite often been seen sunning themselves hereabouts on hot days - being armed with two shovels, a coal pick and my heavy steel-toed boots however, I was not too worried!

When the train arrived, by strange coincidence manned by the same crew we took over from on the previous occasion, we could tell from their expressions that things were back to normal this time. Rosey Jacob, the fireman was quick to assure me that No. 30506 was steaming well, while Dave Wiseman (Junior) quipped, 'Even you should be able to fire it this time, John', then retreated rapidly, before I could throw the dregs from my tea can over him!

As we departed on the first leg, it was clear right from the start that the engine was indeed fully restored to health and we proceeded up the grade to Medstead without any bother. While we stood and awaited our beer swilling passengers, we could make a proper job of fire-cleaning with our newly-restored clinker shovel, but there was one further trauma to befall us before we departed: Bob was using the long pricker to dislodge the clinker down the front end of the box and somehow managed to get the right-angled end stuck down between the firebars! This particular implement is solid steel, some 11 ft long and over an inch in diameter. When fully inserted in the box there was barely a foot protruding through the firehole, and try as we might, we had insufficient

'S15' class No.506 departs Ropley with a rake of Midland Region stock. *P. Goodworth*

Ivatt 2-6-2 tank No.41312 leaving Ropley for Medstead; notice the vintage Morris '8' in the picnic area in the background. *R. Forster*

leverage to dislodge it. After some 15 minutes of sweating and straining with our hands and faces right up by the firehole, Bob was sufficiently worried to get off the engine and ring Ropley shed to let them know we might be a failure. In the end, by dint of rocking the grate open and using a length of scaffold pole found by the track as additional leverage we eventually managed to get it out and sat down red faced and sweating, while we got our breath back.

After this, the trip up the hill was almost an anti-climax - firing four at a time at frequent intervals, the pressure held at 190 against the injector all the way up. As we passed Medstead distant and Bob eased the regulator, the engine even blew off steam, which didn't displease us, as it let our passengers know we were well in command this time. The return leg also went very well and as we stood in Alton for the final run I was feeling quite pleased with myself. Bob was off the engine going round with his oil feeder and I was busying myself with making up the fire again while a crowd of well-lubricated punters stood on the platform observing my efforts. As I had the footplate to myself, I took advantage of the extra room to fire right-handed from the driver's side, although by this time I was pretty well ambidextrous with the shovel. After a minute or two of this, a loud voice came from the platform demanding to know if I was the fireman. I turned round and answered in the affirmative to which my inquisitor replied, 'Well get over your own ruddy side then!' which caused much merriment amongst the audience - many of whom were fellow members of the loco department enjoying a night out. This was Bob Deeth having a little joke at my expense - and I could even afford to see the funny side myself, seeing as the dear old 'S15' had been giving me a decent trip for a change.

Moving on now, we come to the only other working tank engine on the railway, this being an Ivatt class '2' 2-6-2T No. 41312. This locomotive is another ex-Barry scrapyard engine and when it first appeared at Ropley was completely derelict, with nearly all the cab, coal bunker, side tanks and boiler cladding having to be made up from scratch. When I first saw it and had a look at the very small firebox, I had serious doubts as to whether it would be any good working over our very demanding line. Basically an engine needs to be able to get a train moving and then sustain a speed of 25 mph up the 1 in 60 with at least a four-coach train, if it is going to maintain the schedule. I have mentioned before that 'Thomas' has on paper got virtually the same tractive effort as our 'U' class 2-6-0, and is not even very far behind the 'Standard 5' with 23,870 lb. against 26,120, but when it comes to running passenger trains there is no comparison. The 'J94' was designed for shunting duties and soon becomes winded if it is required to run longer distances at any speed - the small boiler being incapable of boiling water fast enough to produce the steam required. Apart from the small grate area, the tractive effort of No. 41312 is also pretty low at a meagre 18,510 lb., so I found it difficult to imagine how it would cope.

As it turned out, my fears were unfounded - the grate may be on the small side but the tube heating area is quite large and of course the engine is superheated which makes a big difference. Superheating incidentally, is a process whereby the steam once it has been produced in the boiler is not taken directly to the cylinders. Instead, it is collected in one half of a header in the smokebox from whence it passes into a large number of small superheater

Bob Cartwright driving *Bodmin* - note full open regulator.   *Author*

Bodmin about to depart from Alresford in 2002 - I hope the driver remembers to wind her into forward gear first!   *Author*

tubes. These in turn pass down the larger diameter superheater flues in the boiler barrel where they are exposed to all the red hot gases passing down from the firebox - tubes within tubes in fact. At the firebox end, the superheater tubes have to do an abrupt U-turn and then go back to the smokebox where they are collected once again in the other half of the header. From here, they enter the main steam pipes which lead to the cylinders. The advantage of superheating is that the steam will not immediately start to condense as soon as it arrives in the cylinders and can therefore do more work before it is exhausted (water droplets are no good at pushing the pistons). Generally speaking, a superheated engine will burn around 25 per cent less coal doing the same job than a similar non-superheated version, which of course is a tremendous advantage.

For my first turn on No. 41312 I was paired up with driver Mike Pearson, who informed me that he had never been on the engine either, so were both on a steep learning curve. The locomotive itself was also on trial - up until this time it had been on running-in turns with just three-coach loads but today we were doing the 'Countryman' dining train with four, so it was a first for all concerned. Mike was obviously a little apprehensive about our prospects and told me not to worry about blowing off steam prior to departure, as he wanted me to ensure we had a full pot and a full head of steam before we started. In the event, everything went off very well, and the little engine showed us it had plenty of guts. Because of the small firebox, it is not possible to stuff nearly as much coal in before you start the trip as you would on a bigger engine, which of course means that much more has to be fired when running - I find it more enjoyable doing this anyway. I soon found that 'little and often' really was the best policy with this engine and kept my firing down to three or four shots at very frequent intervals. This seemed to do the trick and I had little difficulty in keeping the steam pressure up above 180 psi which is where it needed to be - anything less than this and the speed would soon start to fall away. The small wheels gave the impression that the engine was going faster than it really was, which added to the fun and all in all we had a good day out.

Compared to 'Thomas', the cab is nice and roomy, with all the controls conveniently placed. My only real dislike is that the bunker doors open straight onto the cab floor, instead of onto a shovelling plate like most tender engines, so that there is always a mess of coal on the floorboards when running.

Over time I have become quite a fan of the little Ivatt - there is lot more finesse required in firing it compared with some of the bigger engines, which in turn means a greater sense of satisfaction when you pull off a really good run. By comparison, all you need with a Bulleid Pacific is the ability to withstand the heat and the stamina to build up a whacking big fire at the back end before you start each trip, then, when you get away, you splash a dozen shots over the thinner places in the middle and down the front. Having done most of the required coal heaving before you leave the platform, you can probably then sit down comfortably on your seat and watch the beast make steam for the rest of the trip - the real skill with one of these is to judge exactly the right time to stop firing, to ensure that the engine doesn't blow off steam all the way on the downhill run!

Having got round to the subject of Bulleid again, it is time to move on to the final engine in this chapter which is No. 34016 *Bodmin*, our rebuilt 'West Country' class Pacific. I have mentioned this locomotive a few times in the

Rebuilt Bulleid Pacific. This one is 'Merchant Navy' class No. 35005 *Canadian Pacific* being prepared for a main line run. GWR 'King' No. 6024 just visible to left. *Author*

A visiting tank engine in 2004 was Beattie 2-4-0 well tank (the water tank is between the frames) dating back to 1874. *Gwen Cartwright*

previous chapters as being the unhappy skeleton that occupied the middle road of the shed for so many years. Finally, in 1999, the funding finally became available to really get cracking on the rebuild, which then took place very rapidly. By New Year 2000, the boiler was back in the frames and the locomotive was completed and steam tested at the end of May - truly a remarkable achievement by all concerned. My own humble contribution to the project was a set of 12 steam atomisers for the lubrication system, together with their six distribution blocks. These I machined up on my lathe at home, as by this time I had moved back to Canterbury permanently and therefore did not get down to the shed nearly as much as in my Cranleigh days.

Virtually as soon as the locomotive was run in, it was immediately passed for main line running and worked a whole series of steam specials to Canterbury and Salisbury throughout the rest of the year. These 'Cathedrals Express' runs proved to be very successful and brought in some much needed revenue for the railway, although there were some complaints from the volunteers that it meant that they were being denied the chance to run the engine over our own line for much of the time. For myself, living in Canterbury, I was quite often able to meet the train in Canterbury West station, where I could assist with coaling and oiling the engine during the stopover period - and I can assure you that oiling the middle engine is no picnic where there is no pit to work from. The clasp brakes prevent access from between the wheels, which means that the only way in is to start at the front end and wriggle face down over the sleepers all the way back to the middle driving wheel, negotiating the brake rigging *en route* and trying to avoid all the puddles of oil and drips of hot water on the way! Having got there, you then have to climb up over the slippery frame stretchers and connecting rod etc. to get at the various oiling points - no wonder some drivers preferred the original engines.

On one occasion when this train was running, I received an urgent phone call from Frank Boait at Ropley to say that the turbo-generator had packed up and that they were sending some spare bits for the governor up in a taxi, if I could meet the train and fit them. Never having seen one of these little contraptions apart before, I was a bit nervous about starting the job, but thanks to the wonders of modern technology for a change, in the shape of my mobile phone, Frank, who had another generator in front of him in the shed was able to talk me through the operation. I have to say that this was not one of the easiest jobs I had ever tackled, as it meant playing with some remarkably small and delicate bits and pieces in the pouring rain, which, if I had dropped them amongst the ballast would have been lost for good.

Apart from one little hiccup, when I realised I had a locking washer left over and had to start again, the job went fairly smoothly and it was very satisfying finally to hear the whine as the generator ran up and the lights came on - by which time the battery on my mobile phone was nearly flat!

I had to wait almost to the end of October 2000 before I was rostered for my first firing turn on *Bodmin*, which I had been looking forward to immensely and when the appointed day came I made sure I turned up bright and early at the shed. After signing on and reading the usual notices, I grabbed the shed key as I was the first man to arrive and made my way down the cinder track to unlock. It was still pitch dark and as I groped my way up to the shed door, I managed to trip over some

Bob Cartwright cooks the breakfast on *Bodmin* in 2002. Everything in the cab gleams - including Bob's boots!

Author

scrap metal and barked my shin, which was a good start to the day. Worse was to follow, as the padlock refused to yield to the key, which then snapped off in the lock! This meant a trip back to the car to collect some breaking and entering equipment in the shape of the biggest screwdriver in my toolbox. The little brass padlock lasted about five seconds in the face of such a brutal instrument wielded by a man in a bad temper and finally I got in and was able to switch on the lights.

Having collected the usual bundle of rags, I went out to find the engine which was parked on the pit road and looking particularly impressive as I walked up alongside the massive driving wheels in the gloom. Having hoisted all my gear up onto the footplate, I climbed aboard to take stock. I was surprised to find there was still 120 lb. of steam on the clock and a full glass of water - I could have had another half-hour in bed! This was due to the new and improved lagging material which had been used between the boiler and the cladding and it was obviously doing a great job of retaining the heat.

After lighting the fire and doing all the usual preparation jobs, there was even time to cook some breakfast before it was time to get away. As it turned out we couldn't move anyway, as No. 30506 which was parked behind us on the pit road was having trouble getting the tender brakes off, so we were blocked in. Bob Deeth, who by now was the locomotive superintendent, was pacing up and down giving black looks as departure time ticked past and we continued to munch our eggs and bacon but there was not a lot we could do about it. Eventually, the offending brakes were freed off and we could escape down the hill to pick up our train.

I am not going to bore you all here with yet another description of how to fire an engine from Alresford to Alton and back, but it will suffice to say that *Bodmin* runs like a sewing machine and it would be a pretty poor man who couldn't make her steam. Bob Cartwright and I were both enjoying our day out but unfortunately, after our first run up from Alton, we found that a large lump of the brick arch had collapsed and fallen into the fire. During the turn round at Alresford, we struggled with the pricker and clinker shovel and eventually managed to manoeuvre it out of the firehole and then down onto the ballast to cool off. We carried on going but on the second trip we lost another piece, so it was decided we had better come off the train before the whole thing fell in.

A week or two later, I got another turn on this engine, again with Bob as my mate for the first half of the day, after which he had to go back to his real job - driving for South West Trains! He was relieved by Geoff Bailey, now one of our footplate inspectors, so I was trying to be on best behaviour. I managed to provide Geoff with all the steam he required and blew off only once - at which he remarked, somewhat tongue in cheek I thought, that perhaps I had fired about two shovels too many, and as that was the only criticism to come my way during the day, I felt quite satisfied.

Having now fired an example of both rebuilt and original forms of Bulleid Pacific, I can tell you that there is a lot less hard graft required to keep *Bodmin* in steam compared with *Swanage* for the same sort of work, and also that the cab seems a lot cooler - probably due to the new lagging. Although I can accept that the originals had more charisma and certainly put up the occasional outstanding performance, if I had to do this job every day for a living, I would pick a rebuild every time.

Gresley 'A4' Pacific No. 60007 *Sir Nigel Gresley* runs into Ropley in 1996. David Shepherd's '9F' class 2-10-0 No. 92203 *Black Prince* behind and wheeldrop excavations in front.   *Author*

The other end of 'Sir Nigel' in 1996 - note the circular window at the end of the tender passageway.   *Author*

Chapter Nine

Gresley's Masterpiece

In common with most other steam railways, the Mid-Hants has from time to time played host to a number of visiting locomotives, either on an exchange basis or hired in when our own supplies of motive power have been depleted by breakdowns or overhauls. These have varied from an ex-GWR pannier tank, which lasted about one round trip before collapsing under the strain with leaking tubes, to exotic and high-powered machinery such as 'A4' Pacific No. 60007 *Sir Nigel Gresley*, which proved to be a popular and reliable performer. With regard to the latter, I can clearly remember the first time I ever saw one of these magnificent machines - it would have been at Kings Cross *circa* 1957 - and took place during one of my little trainspotting jaunts up to London. I had already spent most of the morning at Paddington, followed by sixpence-worth at a News Theatre watching cartoons before hopping on the tube over to the Cross. By the time I arrived I had therefore missed the flurry of activity around breakfast time, when quite a few expresses departed on their journey north - including of course the 'Flying Scotsman' at 10 am. My chosen viewpoint, in common with a handful of other trainspotters, was on the far end of the platform near the signal box, which commanded a good view across the ends of all the other platforms. Apart from one of Peppercorn's 'A1' Pacifics over at the turntable and an 'N2' tank engine about to depart with a local train, nothing much was happening and we loafed around basking in the sun by the box or eating our sandwiches. Suddenly, the mournful sound of a chime whistle roused us from our torpor, one of the boys called out 'Streak' (as 'A4s' were known to us spotters), and we all moved across to get a better view of whatever was about to emerge from the right-hand portal of Gasworks tunnel - in this case it was No. 60034 *Lord Faringdon* at the head of a long express. As it glided in, several of us raced down the platform and across the footbridge to get a closer look as it came to a stand at the buffer stops. On this occasion the crew seemed to be more interested in leaning out the cab and chatting to the passengers as they walked past (collecting tips maybe?) and none of us got up on the footplate, but I was happy enough just to have seen one at last.

Winding the clock forward some 40 years found me signing on in the shed with my name marked down against a very well-known member of the species - No. 60007 *Sir Nigel Gresley*. If a fortune teller had told me when I left school that one day I would be fireman on an 'A4', I would have suggested that maybe a new crystal ball was required; but there it was in black and white - I was thrilled to bits.

During the 1950s, 'Sir Nigel' was the regular engine of driver Bill Hoole, who was renowned as being one of the hardest hitters at Kings Cross shed. In 1959, whilst pulling an enthusiasts' special for the Stephenson Locomotive Society, he had a serious go at *Mallard's* world speed record - and some say might even have beaten it, had not the footplate inspector told him to ease up. Even so, the speed attained was 112 mph, which was a post-war record for steam. In 1938,

The GWR record breaker *City of Truro* which reputedly was the first engine to reach 100 mph in 1903, seen in Ropley yard in 2005.   *Keith Stockley*

City of Truro running round the train at Alton in 2005.   *Keith Stockley*

when *Mallard* had made her run, she finished it with a badly damaged inside big end but the design had been successfully modified to a Swindon pattern since then, so it was possible - but in my view unlikely, that Bill might have succeeded if he had been left to his own devices.

The problem of attaining really high speeds with a conventional steam engine is that of balancing the moving parts. The pistons and rods of course are going backwards and forwards but this motion steadily changes as you go further down the connecting rod until you reach the big end, where it has become perfectly circular. Weights may be added to the wheels to counteract the out of balance forces generated by the reciprocating parts, but this will make the wheels themselves out of balance. At 120 mph, an 'A4s' driving wheels are going round at more than eight times a second and someone (who would have to be a lot better at maths than me) has proved that at this speed, the wheels actually lift off the track each time the balance weights come round to the top. This in turn means that when they are at the bottom, the force exerted on the rail is at least double what it is with the engine standing still. This force is known as the 'hammer blow effect' and is heartily disliked by the civil engineering department of any railway who will have to repair the damage it does to the track and bridges. For this reason, a compromise has to made with engine balancing and it is usual to have no more than 50 per cent of the reciprocating masses balanced. Even with this precaution, the hammer blow can still be very considerable and was one of the main factors to be taken into account when setting speed limits during steam days. In my view, *Mallard's* world record was probably very close to the absolute maximum possible for a standard gauge reciprocating steam locomotive and is therefore likely to remain forever unbeaten.

Diesel and electric locomotives of course don't have any problems of this kind. The traction motors and axles are devoid of any reciprocating parts and will therefore remain perfectly balanced at any speed, which is why the TGV can hurtle through France at over 200 mph. As this speed is attained by a man sitting in a comfortable air-conditioned cab, who has little more to do than observe the signals and press a button every so often to prove he is still awake, I am afraid it means that the spectacle in my view, is devoid also of any excitement.

Whilst on the subject of steam engines and speed, there is one other record that is worth a mention, which is that of the Great Western Railway's *City of Truro*, for which a speed of 102.3 mph was claimed in 1903. Many pundits have dismissed this claim out of hand and it has to be said that compared with *Mallard*, the GWR engine looks as if it should be in a museum (which it is normally). But if we examine the two records, there are a few points that make the claim seem to be quite feasible and these are as follows: *City of Truro* has the same size driving wheels as *Mallard*; it was pulling a lighter train than *Mallard* and it was going down a steeper hill than *Mallard*. Although *City of Truro* may look archaic, it was actually quite an advanced engine for its time and had a superheated boiler and long travel valves - which were pioneered by its designer George Jackson Churchward. Although it is not streamlined, its frontal area is a good deal less than *Mallard* and the air resistance for an engine at 102 mph is 52 per cent less than for the same engine at 126 mph anyway (it increases as the square of the speed). From the technical viewpoint therefore, I think the record claim is entirely justified. The one thing that is in question is the method of timing; whereas *Mallard* was hauling a dynamometer car with extremely accurate recording equipment, *City of Truro* was being recorded by a country vicar whose hobby was train timing, armed with nothing more than a pair of stop watches reading to one tenth of a second. Much is made of the figure 102.3, as if this was in some way less creditable than if the claim had been a plain 102. Well, I can tell you exactly how this speed was obtained - it is simply what you would get if the time between ¼ mileposts was 8.8 seconds (remember from Chapter One that you divide into 900). As stop watches of the day were certainly accurate to one tenth of a second, I don't have a problem with this. For the locomotive not to have exceeded the magic 100, the vicar would have had to be in error by two-tenths, which I think is unlikely - to be this far out would mean missing the post by 30 ft when pressing the button. In any case, we don't quibble about any of the early world records in athletics or motor racing, which were all timed in the same way up until about 50 years ago.

Having completed that little digression on the subject of speed records, it is time to return to the present narrative. With my name in the signing-on book and the notices read, I wandered off down to the yard to find the engine. It was standing on the pit road looking huge and elegant. Few locomotives are ever likely to make such an impression as one of these, which is why they appeared so often in advertisements of the art deco period whenever speed and grace needed to be depicted - and more recently in the titles of the 'Hercule Poirot' detective series on television. When first built, the valve gear was covered at the sides by steel valances which had a straight bottom edge but this was removed during World War II for ease of maintenance. In my opinion, the gently curved running plate down the line of the boiler with the long rods now fully exposed is an even more graceful arrangement.

When I climbed aboard, my first impression of the cab was that there was plenty of room but that it was rather gloomy, due to the flexible rubber sheet that completely covered the gap between engine and tender. Both driver and fireman are provided with comfortable bucket seats, which look as if they are actually meant to be sat upon, making a pleasant change from the Spartan bits of plank to be found on so many other engines. Another unusual feature of the engine is the reversing screw, which is mounted vertically beside the driver's seat, instead of horizontally in front of him, which is the more usual arrangement - I seem to recall that it needed to be turned anti-clockwise to put the engine in fore gear which is also the opposite to what you would expect. The cut-off indicator consists of an engraved brass strip mounted on the back of the boiler with a pointer travelling up and down it.

On the front of the huge tender on the fireman's side is a small door, which is the opening into the corridor that can connect with the front coach of the train. This was an innovation by Gresley, to enable crews to be changed with the engine in motion during the non-stop runs between London and Edinburgh. I had a peek inside and found the corridor to be the repository for various spare parts, tools and other locomotive bricabrac, which made it impossible to get through - but it was plain enough to see that the passage is extremely narrow and I can imagine the more portly drivers would have had quite a squeeze getting through.

I spent a minute or two sitting in the driver's seat and looking out over that long curved running plate, while trying to imagine what Joe Duddington and Tommy Bray must have felt like back in 1938 on the day of the world record run, as they launched *Mallard* down Stoke bank like a 160 ton torpedo. My daydreams of the East Coast main line were interrupted by a shout from below announcing the arrival of my driver and I hopped down from my lofty perch to commence preparing 'Sir Nigel' for the road. First thing to do was to check the water, so I opened up the two Klinger pattern gauge glasses which are situated high up on the back of the boiler. We had about ⅔ of a glass and some 30 lb. of steam still on the clock, so we could take our time over the 'prep'.

Instead of the usual grate fingers which can be rocked back and forth to drop the fire, as fitted to most of our own engines, this one has a rather small square section of grate under the brick arch, which is hinged and can be wound down about 45 degrees; this leaves a gap through which the remaining ash and clinker can be shoved using the fire irons. After spending several minutes on the ground beside the firebox searching fruitlessly for the means of operating this particular gubbins, I decided to try my luck in the cab instead and eventually found a small shaft with a square end sticking up near the fireman's seat and a matching handle to wind it with. This did the business and I could then get stuck and dispose of the fire with the clinker shovel, rake and bent dart applied through the firehole.

The firehole door is of a pattern peculiar to the LNER and consists of a large oval main door hinged on the left-hand side, which can be hooked back out of the way when the fire irons are being employed but which remains closed when the engine is being fired on the road. To fire the engine, there is a much smaller semi-circular opening in the lower half of the main door, with a flap, which can be swung inwards to provide room for the shovel. This flap can be set in the required position by a kind of ratchet affair so that it can be used to regulate the amount of secondary air getting in to the fire. The opening is very small compared to most engines and the LNER had a special shovel designed for it, with a long handle and a small blade, quite heavily cranked, to facilitate firing to the back corners. When I first saw this arrangement I thought it looked very awkward, but in practice it proved otherwise; the draught through the small opening being so strong that it was really unnecessary to do much more than gently swing the shovel in the general direction required and the inrushing air would do the rest. To hit the back corners was a little more difficult, it being necessary to poke the shovel all the way in past the flap before being flicked sideways. My only real criticisms were that the small shovel needed twice as many shots to fill the box as with the LMS or Southern versions and also that any of the larger lumps, that would have been ideal for the back corners, would have to be broken to get them through the small opening - (our friends from the A4 Society being most insistent that the main door was not to be opened when firing on the road).

Having cleaned the fire and restored the drop grate, the next thing to do was check the smokebox, which immediately presented another problem. That beautifully shaped front end (reputedly designed in a wind tunnel) appeared to be devoid of any means of opening it. Eventually I spotted another square ended shaft sticking out by the left-hand cylinder, which could be turned using the same handle that dropped the grate. This caused the front panel to lift up and exposed the real smokebox door within - this in turn being opened by the usual two handles in the middle. Having got into the inner sanctum, I was confronted by the complexities of the Kylchap exhaust arrangement (named after its inventors - Kylala and Chapelon), with its twin blast pipes, various fancy-shaped cones and baffles surrounding the base of the chimney and with the steam pipes snaking round the outsides - I can't pretend that I knew how it was all supposed to work but as there were no signs of leaks or anything obviously coming adrift, I shut it all up again and returned to the cab to light the fire.

While I was doing this, I was joined on the footplate by the burly figure of Roger Barker of the A4 Society, who was staying with the locomotive as a 'minder' during its sojourn on our railway. Roger knows the locomotive inside out and is a mine of information on the best way of operating it and all the little idiosyncrasies that give an engine its character. One nugget that comes my way is to avoid braking hard when going backwards - even if the boiler pressure is well below the red line, the surge of water back down the boiler barrel as the engine decelerates, impacts under the safety valves and will cause them to lift. Now 'A4' safeties must be about the noisiest valves fitted to any engine and are installed right at the back end of the boiler, so this sudden explosion right above your head is liable to cause the crew together with anyone else standing within about 100 yards to jump out of their skin!

I asked Roger what he thought of operating this greyhound of the iron road over our little railway, expecting a polite but possibly rather patronising reply. I was surprised therefore when he said he thought that four round trips over our line with six coaches was as demanding as a main line run with 12 on and certainly required a very high level of boiler control if one was to provide enough steam for the climbs while ensuring the engine didn't blow off steam in the stations - later on he even expressed the same sentiments in *Steam Railway* magazine. This I think was quite a compliment on the standard of enginemanship generally on the Mid-Hants and scotches a lot of the criticism we get from self proclaimed experts, who think that operating a preserved line such as ours is little more than grown-ups playing trains.

With the fire burning nicely and the all the other chores completed, there was time to give 'Sir Nigel' a bit of a clean to present its best appearance to the waiting public. This was 'Thomas' week once again and as an 'A4' looks nothing like any of the characters in the books, we would not be running with any inappropriate face hung on the front. Instead, Roger supplied us with a proper headboard: 'The Flying Scotsman' no less, which is something I will be able to boast about to my grandchildren! Finally, when it was our turn to move, we collected the token and glided off down to Alresford to pick up our train. You will note that I used the word 'glide' here, which was very appropriate, seeing as this wonderful machine rode like a coach, and was virtually free of the knocks and other mechanical noises that usually accompany a steam locomotive in motion. The cab itself however was not so quiet, especially when the injectors were in use, because the combined steam and delivery valves are installed on the backhead of the boiler right in front of you, while the brake ejector is also in the cab and was a bit on the noisy side.

As Alresford station appeared round the final bend we gave a long wail on that wonderful chime whistle to let everyone know we were coming. These whistles were modelled on the American pattern and consist of a thin brass cylinder divided longitudinally into three sections, each stopped at a different height to give the three different notes (C, F and A flat for the benefit of any musicians reading this), the steam being blown upwards through an annular slot against the lips of the three mouthpieces cut into the bottom of the cylinder.

We had a six-coach train waiting for us down in Alresford, well filled with parents and their children, many of them waving 'Thomas' flags at us as we crept down and buffered up. Some of the children asked us what had happened to 'Gordon' (the blue express engine from the books), so the story line we put out was that 'Sir Nigel' had come to the railway to help out because 'Gordon' had broken down and had been sent away for repair.

My main impressions of the locomotive from the footplate point of view were firstly, how surefooted it was for a Pacific - on all our trips out of Alton, as soon as we had negotiated the point work and curves leaving the station, the regulator was whacked wide open without ceremony and the engine just took off like the proverbial scalded cat, with no hint of a slip. The other big surprise was how easy it was to fire through that small half door and how free the boiler was for steam. On one occasion, we had to stand at Alton for nearly an hour and the fire had actually gone out over several square feet of grate, while the pressure stood at around 210 psi. On Roger's advice, however, I did nothing to the fire until about 10 minutes before departure, then rapidly filled the holes and the back corners. The pressure started coming round so fast that I thought even then that I might have started too early and was glad to see the green flag and get away without a blow-off.

The climb that followed was a real eye-opener as to the power of these wonderful engines. As we were quite late getting away, the driver (who shall remain nameless) had obviously decided this was a good excuse to really open up and regain some time - or at least have some fun in the attempt! Coming over Butts Junction, the regulator was opened up full and the cut-off left on 40%, with the result that we reached 54 mph up the 1 in 60, before having to shut off for Medstead - the fastest I have ever been up the hill.

At this point it is worth while mentioning that the Mid-Hants Railway operates under a Light Railway Order, which is part of a rather archaic piece of legislation dating back to 1896, although earlier legislation had permitted 'light railways'. The Act allowed small branch lines to be built on the cheap, with lighter track, tighter curves, ground frames instead of signal boxes and various other concessions. There were also some restrictions as well, one of which was a speed limit of 25 mph. The Mid-Hants did not originally fall under this category and was built to main line standards - in fact it was frequently used as an alternative route to Southampton and Bournemouth when the normal line through Basingstoke was closed for engineering work. When it was re-opened

Gresley 'A4' No. 60019 *Bittern* which was restored on the Mid-Hants Railway between 2001 and 2007 stands outside the shed at Ropley in 2007.   *Author*

Bittern stands in Ropley yard in 2008.   *Author*

in private hands however, in common with nearly all other preserved railways, its permit to operate was granted under the conditions of the Light Railway Order, together with the speed restriction, even though the track is still maintained to the highest standards and is capable of being operated at much higher speeds. I have travelled on some other lines where the track was more like an inferior colliery siding and the 25 mph limit in fact seems to be over generous but the Mid-Hants is not like this.

It is possible to negotiate with the Health and Safety Executive (HSE) and the Railway Inspectorate to have the limit raised but this would mean spending considerable amounts of money to pay for the investigation and inspection process and in any event, there is little point in trying to run much faster because the passengers would not have time to enjoy the ride. This being said, when a driver is faced with the sort of gradients we have on the Mid-Hants, he is not normally going to pussy foot around keeping the speed down to 25 mph across the Butts on a rainy day with three miles of 1 in 60 awaiting him, so the speedometer would frequently be allowed to stray into the thirties. This happy situation prevailed until 2005, when the HSE went out and bought themselves hand-held GPS (global positioning by satellite) gear, which enabled them to travel on the trains and do spot checks on the speeds. Several railways apart from the Mid-Hants were found to be exceeding the speed limit and various wrists got slapped. The upshot of it all is that the 25 mph limit is now strictly observed and the railway has even bought itself a GPS to do its own checks - and also to calibrate the speedometers on the locomotives. Without being allowed to get a run at the banks this has made it a lot more difficult to operate the railway and in some respects less safe rather than more so. When running tender first downhill for example, the driver is spending nearly the whole time looking at the speedometer and brake gauges rather than at the road, for fear of breaking the speed limit by a few miles per hour.

The usual procedure at Alresford is for all trains to arrive in and depart from the up platform, which is adjacent to the exit to the car park and all the station amenities, thereby precluding the need for passengers to negotiate the footbridge. When the engine is detached, it runs forward over the crossover points and then back round the train. The starting signal at the end of the down platform is usually left at danger until the locomotive is quite close before being pulled off. There is normally no reason why this couldn't be done earlier, but the signalman is no doubt mindful of the foot crossing, which will be just behind the back of the coaches and uses this method to slow the engines down, just in case someone foolishly decides to use it as an engine is approaching.

On this particular occasion, 'Sir Nigel' was running back round the train and approaching the starting signal, which the driver was expecting to be cleared, but for some reason the signalman did not pull it off as usual and we had to brake rather hard to avoid running past it at danger. You may be able to guess what happened next: the water surge back down the boiler caused those wretched safety valves to lift with a noise like the crack of doom, even though the pressure was well below the normal blowing off point. What an awful racket! Anyone passing with a weak constitution could have had heart failure, while both me and the driver were left white-faced with shock. Roger Barker, who was sitting in the fireman's seat just turned round with a bit of a grin and a 'told you so' kind of expression. You can believe it or not but this was the first time (regrettably not the last, however), that I had ever had an engine blow off steam in Alresford station!

Despite the fact that the railway was built at least a hundred years before most of the houses surrounding the station at Alresford, the railway still gets plenty of complaints from these residents about the noise and smoke from engines, so we do our level best to avoid both - not always successfully I might add. Some years later I was on *Bodmin* standing at the head of our train in Alresford; the boiler was well under control, or so I thought, with a bit of water space left and 235 psi on the clock. Departure was only a couple of minutes away and the pressure was creeping up slowly; at 240 psi the safeties lifted with a nerve shattering roar - 10 psi early. Bob Deeth was on the platform pretty well beside the engine when this happened and gave me one of his famous black looks - all I could do was to mumble, 'The valves are 10 pounds light Bob', which seemed to do little to pacify him. The following day at the same time, found me at Alresford once again, this time on another visiting 'A4' No. 60009 *Union of South Africa*. By some terrible coincidence, these safeties also lifted 10 lb. early and once again Bob Deeth was on the platform to witness it. I cringed away on the other side of the footplate and left the driver to lean out of the cab to face the music - 'You tell him', I said, 'He's never going to believe me!'

Plenty of atmosphere in this shot (it's the exhaust from the generator). The gentleman in the middle is David Butcher - ex mainline fireman at Kings Cross, flanked by Bob Cartwright and the author – the latter looking a little warm.   *Gwen Cartwright*

Chapter Ten

Learner Driver

Many small boys of my generation, if they were asked about what they wanted to be when they grew up, might well have replied 'engine driver', 'fireman' (the sort that put out fires!) or 'jet pilot', and of these, engine driver would probably have been the most popular; I wonder what the answers would be now - footballer or rock star perhaps? Engine driver was certainly my choice and remained so right up until I left school and realised that there weren't going to be any steam engines left to drive.

The idea still stuck in my brain, however, along with various other pipedreams such as flying a Spitfire, climbing the Matterhorn, driving the Le Mans 24 hour race, cycling from Land's End to John O'Groats (I might still have a bash at this) and various other over-ambitious fancies. The strange thing was, that when I joined the Mid-Hants, and becoming a driver became an actual possibility, I virtually forgot all about it at first. There were a couple of reasons for this: in the first place I really enjoyed being a fireman - the mental challenge of controlling the boiler and trying to keep one jump ahead of the engine, together with the physical exercise which I certainly needed, made every visit most enjoyable. The second reason, was that my perception of the driver's job was that there was not much to it - he had all the responsibility for running the trains safely of course, but for the actual driving bit, one handle made it go and another one made it stop - or so I thought, and during my first few years on the railway, when all the driving I did was confined to returning light engines to the shed after their day's work, nothing much happened to disabuse me of this simplistic theory.

After I had been paired up with Bob Cartwright for a couple of years, however, the powers that be decided that I should start driver training, with Bob as my instructor. I was happy enough by now to go along with this, as after about eight years on the shovel, some of my contemporaries had already been passed out for driving and I was beginning to wonder if I might miss the boat. Also, I was now aged 55 and a full day's firing was starting to seem like hard work!

Before this all happened it was deemed necessary to send out a footplate inspector with us, to watch me drive a trip under Bob's guidance to see whether he (Bob) was competent to be an instructor, which I have to say I thought was quite ridiculous - Bob is after all a driving instructor for South West Trains on the main rail network! At any rate, all was found to be satisfactory and the next 2½ years, during which Bob and I split our turns, with each of us doing a spell at each job, turned out to be my happiest times on the railway.

I mentioned above about the one handle to make it go and the one to make it stop - well, it's the one that makes it stop that separates the men from the boys. A popular saying amongst footplatemen is that 'Any fool can start an engine but it takes a driver to stop it'. What they really mean is that it takes a driver to stop it in the right place - and of course to know where the right place is. Trains vary in length and the stopping points at each station will be different according to how many coaches there are. There are some points where it is vital that the train does not stop short: for instance, at Alton, where half a coach length before the mark will leave the tail of the train foul of the points, so the engine will be unable to run-round it for the return trip. In this unhappy circumstance, the driver will have to go cap in hand to the guard to arrange to have all the doors shut again and the passengers warned that the train is about to move - just to shift that extra 20 feet or so. At Alresford, you have the opportunity of doing it wrong either way: too far past the six-coach mark and the train will be foul of the points at that end as you run round, while if you stop short, you will find the engine will already be past the starting signal at the end of the platform after it has run round and hooked on again. This in turn means it will be sitting on a track circuit, which tells the signalman the section is occupied and will prevent him from pulling the signal off to let you depart, when the time comes. He will now have to come down from his cosy signal box and stand at the signal post to give you a green flag instead, as authority for you to continue past it at danger - and you will be very unpopular if is raining!

Stopping right for water requires an even more precise stop: if you miss by more than about three or four feet either way, the hose at the water column will not reach the tender filling hole. Once again, the train cannot be moved after it has stopped, because of the danger to passengers getting on and off, so the engine will just have to wait until the next opportunity, providing the driver judges there is enough water left to do so in safety. To complicate matters even further, our engines make regular forays out onto the main line to work steam specials - and are not always facing the same way when they come back. This means that the driver now has to learn a completely new set of stopping marks to accommodate his altered perspective.

I have explained in an earlier chapter how the actual vacuum brake system works, basically by admitting air to the train pipe through the driver's application valve, which will push up all the brake pistons throughout the train and apply the brakes. If the locomotive is steam braked, the rise in train pipe pressure acts on a diaphragm within the steam brake control valve in the cab and applies the engine brakes as well. The problem is that the air going in takes time to reach all the way down the train, so there will always be a delayed action effect when the brakes are applied. Similarly, when the brake handle is put to the release position, there is an even longer delay before all the air can be sucked out of the system again and the brakes come off. If an emergency application is made by dropping all the vacuum in one hit, then the braking is virtually immediate, with the engine brake coming on first, followed in sequence by the coaches down the train - and any standing passengers are likely to end up on the floor! For most purposes, however, when running at the sedate speeds of a typical preserved railway, it is unnecessary to drop the vacuum below 10 in. from the normal 21 in. and the delayed action effect is very noticeable. The usual beginner's mistake therefore, is to make a gentle brake application as the train approaches the platform, then, seeing that nothing much seems to be happening, he makes a bigger one. At this point he suddenly finds that the train is slowing down too much, so he attempts to release the brake again but because of the time it takes for the ejectors to suck enough air out of the system, the train finishes up stopping short - been there, done that!

Being an old fashioned 'nuts and bolts' type of engineer, I have never had much trouble in learning how to operate any new machine or mechanical device I was presented with - old cars with unusual pedal and gearbox arrangements, steam rollers, turbines and giant marine diesel engines were all taken in my stride; it came therefore as an unpleasant surprise to find that I was absolutely hopeless on the vacuum brake. Nearly all my station stops at first were accompanied by yells from Bob to 'blow the brakes off' pretty well as soon as I had made an application, together with a frantic grab at the regulator by me to keep the train moving.

Occasionally I would achieve a couple of decent stops in a row and would begin to imagine I was getting the measure of it but then the next one would be half a coach out, which would knock my confidence right back to square one. Bob, to his eternal credit, never showed a flicker of the exasperation he must have been feeling and assured me that it would come to me eventually. On most of my early lessons, the concentration required left me mentally exhausted after just one round trip and only too happy to get back on the shovel again. As we only averaged a turn together every two or three weeks, it took a long time before I started to get the hang of it all.

I tried various things in an attempt to make things easier - firstly I thought that if I ran down the platform very slowly at not much more than walking pace, it would give me more time to think and judge the distances. The problem with this idea was that the braking required now became even more delicate; the slightest bit too much brake and the train would stop short before you could blow it off again. OK then, how about trying it a bit faster; In this case the application could be coarser but now the thinking time was reduced and I would sometimes finish up in a bit of a panic and having to make a very heavy application to finally stop the train, which was a bit rough on the passengers.

In the end it did come to me, but it was not like learning to ride a bike, where one day you can't do it and then suddenly you can. (Tip here for parents teaching their children to ride: throw away any stabiliser wheels, remove the pedals and set the saddle low enough so that their feet easily touch the ground, then just get them to scoot about using their feet for propulsion until they get the hang of balancing the bike – a gentle slope to coast down is best. When they become proficient, put the pedals back; all three of my children learnt to do it this way in an afternoon.)

With my braking it was a much more gradual process but there were two things that seemed to be the most help. The first was to learn to 'rub the brake', that is to drop the vacuum by just three or four inches, which was enough to take up the slack in the system and bring the blocks gently into contact with the wheels. If this position could be maintained as the train ran in, then any further application would have an almost immediate effect. It was quite tricky at first, as you would be spending so much time looking at the brake gauge to maintain the desired vacuum that you could barely afford to look out the cab window to see where you actually were! The second thing was a methodical approach; always try and be at the same speed at the same place. The prescribed speed for

British heavy freight engine: BR Standard class '9F' 2-10-0 No. 92212 in Ropley yard in 2005. I would back one of these against an 'S160' anyday. *P. Goodworth*

Newly-painted '9F' class No.92212 poses for the photograph at Medstead. *Steve Walters*

exchanging the tokens as you run into a station is 10 mph and so I tried to ensure that was exactly what I was doing on each approach. As I ran into a station then, I would attempt to just rub the brake all the way down the platform until I judged the time was right to make the final application, following this, put the handle back to the release position a few yards before the train stopped; if I got it right, the brakes would be almost off again as the train finally came to a stand, which would mean a nice gentle stop.

By these means and with Bob's continued good-natured encouragement and advice, I finally began to get a grip on it. From being pleased at first if I could stop inside half a coach length of the desired spot, I could usually get it now to within a yard or two, which was quite good enough. Bob was obviously sufficiently confident that he even let me have a go at stopping for water at Ropley when we were out once on '9F' No. 92212; I rewarded his trust immediately with a clear miss! Fortunately, the tender on that engine held enough water so that we could get it next time and Bob showed me how it should be done.

Most of my errors now were not that I was missing the point I was aiming at but that the aiming point itself was wrong. Coming in to Medstead for instance in the down direction, I stopped a six-coach train once with the end of the first coach right opposite the end of the platform - just right I thought, until Bob gently pointed out that the tail of the train had not cleared the points into the loop and was foul of the up line! No harm was done because the up train was held at the starting signal anyway, but it did mean the poor old signalman now had to walk down the track to pass behind our train to get back to his box with our token, instead of using the boarded crossing right opposite it. Another mistake was to stop the train in what you thought was the correct place, only to find that you had left the engine with the chimney or safety valves right under a footbridge - not good for public relations, especially if the fireman allowed the engine to blow off steam or make black smoke! By and large though, I was beginning to make a reasonable job of it and actually started to enjoy myself again, which was a relief.

Shortly after I had started driver training, it was the annual steam gala weekend, with a number of visiting engines in attendance, including GWR 'King' class 4-6-0 No. 6024 *King Edward I* and '9F' No. 92212. We were rostered out on *Bodmin* and it was decided that as a special treat for the visiting steam fans, each of these engines would work one round trip with a 10-coach train, so that they could be really opened and give some decent exhaust noise for the tape recorders. To make things even more interesting, a speed limit of 10 mph was imposed across Butts Junction, to prevent any of the engines getting a flying start at the bank.

Bob was going to drive this one, which was only sensible in view of my virtual total lack of experience at that time and I was more than happy to have a bash on the shovel to see if I could provide the steam for a job of this kind. When it was our turn to run, Bob was very strict in his observance of the 10 mph speed restriction - in fact we were nearly down to walking pace coming over the bridge. Then he looked across at me and enquired if I was 'all set' and upon receiving my thumbs up, gave me a big grin and proceeded to heave the

Fireman Rod Tye is obviously having a good day on '9F' No.92212.   *Author*

The author getting a driving lesson on No. 92212, about to depart from Medstead for Ropley.

Gwen Cartwright

The power and the glory Great Western style - 'King' class 4-6-0 No. 6024 *King Edward I* pulls out of Ropley in 2003.

B. Zehetmayr

GWR 'King' class 4-6-0 No. 6024 *King Edward I* and SR 'Merchant Navy' class 4-6-2 No. 35005 *Canadian Pacific* side by side in Ropley yard.   *Author*

regulator wide open and then wound the reverser steadily into full gear! Anybody who thinks that Bulleids have a quiet exhaust should have heard us then - the barks from the chimney were incredible and we were sending a solid column of smoke vertically upwards, at least 40 feet into the air.

What amazed me was that the engine took all this without even the hint of a slip and we accelerated our train steadily away. I had put on a whacking big fire before we started and now commenced to feed it steadily, throwing most of the coal just inside the doors onto the slope and directing the rest sideways into the back corners as best I could. The boiler responded immediately and was soon blowing off even against the injector, which proved once and for all what magnificent steam raisers these Bulleid boilers are. Eventually we worked our train up to 32 mph by the summit, which I think was a very commendable effort - we really couldn't have done much more as the reverser at no time was brought back below 60 per cent cut-off. The 'King' turned out to be fastest at 46 mph but we heard that it had cheated by going over Butts at 18 mph, while No. 92212 reached 42 mph. As both these engines have tractive efforts in excess of 40,000 lb. against our 27,715, it made our achievement all the more remarkable.

The 'King' was only on the railway for a week or so and we never got to have a proper go on it, although we did manage a lunchtime relief once, which meant we could take it from Ropley to Alresford and back while the regular crew got their dinner. It certainly was a magnificent machine and the army of minders and assistants that went everywhere with it ensured that it was cleaned to perfection; no oily rags rubbed over the paintwork Mid-Hants style for this engine - they actually used car polish instead!

In common with the Southern 'Lord Nelsons' it had the longest firebox of any engine to run on British Railways and it took a mighty swing on the shovel to get any down the front of the box I can tell you. That being said, the chief minder warned us against putting too much down there, as the steaming would be adversely affected if it got choked up under the brick arch. The biggest and heaviest fire iron I have ever seen, in the shape of an enormously long rake was carried on the engine and could be employed to pull some of the fire back toward the door if this ever happened. For my little spell of firing, which was basically just to make the fire up once down at Alresford, I spurned the Great Western shovel I was offered and used my own instead - the GWR one seemed to be all shovel and no handle - a most unwieldy weapon in fact. Such was the insularity of the GWR, however, that thousands of firemen had used the same type back since Churchward's days and probably thought it was the best in the world!

A few weeks later and Bob and I were booked out on another visitor from the Great Western, in the shape of No. 5029 *Nunney Castle*. We were not cheered by the news that the fireman on the previous turn had struggled for steam all day and had finished one run with only 80 lb. on the clock and the water nearly gone! He was lucky that Great Western engines have an engine driven vacuum pump to keep the brakes off, or else he would have come to an unscheduled stop somewhere out in the wilds of Chawton Woods!

I managed to exhaust my usual daily quota of swear words in the first 20 minutes aboard this engine, as I struggled with the various fire irons and clinker shovel to clean the fire - no rocking grates or hopper ashpans for the GWR - they did things the hard way right up to the end of steam. At the bigger GWR depots, they employed firedroppers, whose job was solely to clean fires and empty ashpans and smokeboxes. That was all they ever did; no progression to fireman and driver, just disposing of one engine after another as they arrived on shed with boxes full of fire and red hot clinker. It will come as no surprise to find that it was difficult to recruit staff to perform such arduous and dirty work and was yet another reason why steam came to such an abrupt end.

After cleaning the grate and lighting up again, I dropped down into the pit to rake out the two ashpans - one each side of the trailing axle and with a damper at each end through which I had to manoeuvre the rake; this guaranteed that whichever way the wind was blowing you would a facefull of dust before you were finished - more naughty words! During this process, I found that the back of the front ashpan and the front of the rear ashpan were completely choked with ash, which took me nearly a quarter of an hour to clear. This would explain why the previous fireman had such a struggle - perhaps he didn't know the rake had to be applied from four places on this engine! With this vile job finally completed and the dust settled, Bob started to go round with his oil feeder to attend to the scores of oiling points.

After this somewhat lengthy preparation, the day started to look up. *Nunney Castle* proved to be a strong and free steaming engine and stormed up and down the banks in fine style. We had Richard Hardy travelling with us on a footplate pass, a very well known name in railway circles. Starting his career as a premium apprentice at Doncaster works, he went on to become shedmaster at

LNER 'A4' class 4-6-2 No. 60009 *Union of South Africa* approaching Ropley from the west in 2003.

Author

Driver Geoff Bailey and fireman Phil Harding look as if they are enjoying themselves on No. 60009 in 2003.

Author

Woodford, Ipswich and Stewarts Lane, before moving on to more senior management positions. Since retiring, he had written a couple of books including *Steam in the Blood*, a signed copy of which I have on the shelf beside me, as I type my own humble offering. He was also well-known for his love of getting out on the footplates of the engines under his charge and having a go from both sides of the footplate. Today was no different and all three of us each had a spell at driving and firing *Nunney Castle*. Dick Hardy demonstrated that even at age 78, he could still swing a shovel and kept the clock up to the red line, while I did the driving up from Alton and Bob observed. I managed to stop in all the right places and it generally turned out to be a jolly good day.

Another exotic visitor that year was 'A4' Pacific No. 60009 *Union of South Africa*. This was only on the railway for a few days and to ensure fairness, crews were selected by drawing lots. Bob and I struck lucky but unfortunately the engine was stopped with a leaking regulator gland when we turned up for our shift. By dint of a rapid blow down to get rid of the residual boiler pressure and some slightly burned fingers, however, the 'minder' (whose name I forget) and I managed to get the gland repacked in record time. After this we rapidly relit the fire, so that in the end we only missed one round trip. I did not really expect to be given a go at driving this engine and was quite surprised therefore, when the 'minder' stood aside down at Alton for the final trip and motioned me over to the driver's side. Oh boy, did I feel important as I climbed up into the left hand bucket seat and wound the engine into gear for departure. I was brought very rapidly down to earth again as the 'minder' pointed out that the reverser needed to be wound anti-clockwise for forward gear and I was about to depart in the wrong direction! After this unfortunate start, however, I managed to get everything else right and earned a compliment from Bob, who thought I had handled this completely strange locomotive very well. My thoughts about the engine? Tremendous power, a wonderful free steaming boiler and that lovely chime whistle.

'Merchant Navy' Pacific No. 35005 *Canadian Pacific* also came to the railway around this time and is now permanently based here. I had a couple of firing turns on it when it first arrived and was not very impressed. It was a very powerful engine and would climb the banks on around 10 per cent less cut-off than *Bodmin*, but otherwise the extra eight square feet of grate just meant quite a bit more shovelling for the same work, especially when making the fire up before departure. The grate itself was less steeply sloped than on its smaller cousin and therefore needed more coal thrown across the middle and front of the grate, whereas on *Bodmin*, if you had a big heap under the door, then the slope and the blast would take it everywhere else it needed to go.

From the driving point of view, the worst feature of these Bulleids was the brake application valve. This could not be set to give a steady vacuum - as soon as you let go of the handle, the brake was either going on or coming off. If the gland packing around the spindle got a bit tired, then the vibration could cause it to gravitate down to the 'on' position while you were running. The first the driver would know of this, unless he happened to spot it on the brake gauge, was when the speed started to fall off. In this case, he had to very quick off the mark in putting the handle back up to blow it off again and giving the engine

Rebuilt Bulleid 'Merchant Navy' class Pacific No. 35005 *Canadian Pacific* takes water at Ropley.
Author

No. 35005 *Canadian Pacific* heads into the sunset at Ropley. *R. Forster*

the gun, otherwise the train would come to an undignified and unscheduled stop in mid-section. Until the spindle could be repacked, the driver therefore had to keep his hand on the brake the entire time the engine was running; on the downhill sections in order to maintain the required degree of braking and on the uphill parts to avoid an unwanted application - by and large it made hard work of it.

All Bulleid Pacifics are steam braked on the locomotive and vacuum braked on the tender. It is quite easy to move one around the yard on 80 lb. of steam or less with the vacuum brake isolated (you need at least 140 lb. to create a vacuum) but one has to bear in mind when doing this that there are no power brakes on the tender and the steam brake will not have a lot of bite either. I would always have the fireman standing by the handbrake with the slack already wound out of it if I had to move one in this condition. The steam brake is operated by a small lever to the right of the main application valve. Not being fitted with a ratchet to hold it on, it is common practice to find a suitable sized lump of coal to jam it with if you are holding a train by the engine brake alone when waiting for the 'right away'. After a couple of trips using this method I made up a suitably-sized wooden wedge instead, which now lives permanently in my tool bucket.

Compared to the Bulleids, the BR Standard engines have a wonderful brake system. The application valve is mounted on a plinth beside the driver's right hand and moves in the horizontal plane. By giving gentle taps one way or the other it can be set to give any desired vacuum and will pretty much stay put. There is also a graduated steam brake operating on both engine and tender. This has a nice fine ratchet on the handle which can be applied one click at a time; this makes buffering up or running light engine downhill very easy to control. Nos. 73096 and 92212 are definitely my favourite engines to drive, and I am always pleased if I see myself marked down for either of them, just as I had been as a fireman.

Bob, incidentally, still very much enjoys his firing and sometimes we would even argue light heartedly as to whose turn it was to be on the shovel! He is a real swinger when it comes to stoking and is a pleasure to watch in action. He has one particular shot, where the hand on the handle moves deftly sideways at the point of delivery while the one near the blade remains stationary and acts as a fulchrum; this causes the coal to spray out fan wise across the grate - very handy for Bulleids.

I had really enjoyed the time I spent on driver training and was in no hurry to take the driving test, which if I passed, would mean Bob and I would be split up. All good things come to an end, however, and so it was that in October 2004 I was instructed to report at the 'Manor' to take the written examination.

The author applying some oil to *Bodmin*'s big end in 2005.   *Author*

Chapter Eleven

The Other Side of the Footplate

The written exam consisted of two papers of around 20 questions each. There was no time limit on the exam but all questions had to be answered. The first part dealt with the rules and was I thought a real stinker, with several questions along the lines of 'What would you do if such and such a scenario occurred?' Most of these scenarios were ones that I had never come across in practice and so took a considerable amount of head scratching to answer. One I recall went something like this, 'What would you do if you were approaching Ropley in the up direction with a passenger train and the home signal was at danger but the dummy was cleared?' The bottom line here is that dummy signals control shunting movements and not passenger trains, so you would of course stop the train at the home signal and enquire from the signalman what his intentions were. This is what I did in fact write eventually, but not before I had gone into a long screed about this is how the signals would appear if you were coming up light engine and were going on shed - correct, but not what was being asked for! The second part was all questions on the locomotive, both technical and practical. These I found a lot easier but there still seemed to be a lot of writing and it was 3½ hours before I had finished. Almost as soon as I walked out of the 'Manor', thoughts started buzzing round in my brain about the things I should have said and others that would have been better left out but it was too late then, so I just had to stew and await results. In the end, after about a week, Bob Deeth said that I had actually done quite a good paper and was therefore cleared to go on and take the practical, which would consist of preparing an engine and driving one round trip.

The railway is pretty quiet at this time of year and it was not until January that a convenient turn came up. The booked engine was *Bodmin* - just my luck I thought; what with all that inside motion to oil up and the wretched brake handle to contend with. Having read the notices I wandered off down to the engine and collected the oil cans. Oiling up a rebuilt Bulleid Pacific is a dirty and lengthy process and goes something like this. Firstly the easy bit: 10 corks and three oil boxes down each side of the engine, plus the expansion link die blocks and a splash on each of the tender axlebox horn guides. Then climb up onto the running plate and fill four small oil boxes each side which feed the driving axleboxes and horn guides. While still up here, top up the mechanical lubricators and give each of the priming handles a few turns. Back down on the ground again and the next items on the list are the trailing truck and tender axleboxes. The tender ones can be accessed by simply loosening the two nuts that hold on the cover; this can then be lifted off to allow a syringe to be inserted to suck out any water - and it is amazing how often you will find some. Finally use the oil pumper to top them up again. The trailing truck, however, requires two split pins to be extracted and the nuts screwed right off before the covers can be removed - the split pins being invariably well mangled and difficult to pull out.

Now for the dirty bit:- get down in the pit, preferably with an assistant remaining outside to operate the oil pumper. At this stage of the game you may find that your feet are getting wet. Although the pit is equipped with a pump to get rid of the water, every time an engine arrives it will dump the contents of its ashpan, which may cause a blockage and prevent the water from running back to it. So the first job may well be to get a shovel and do a bit of dam busting! Having completed this little chore the next will be to obtain a suitably sized box spanner and partially undo all the driving and coupled wheel axlebox drain plugs to check for water; if there is any it will run out first. When the oil starts to appear, tighten them up again - while doing this, the oil will of course be running down the spanner and up your arm as well! When completed, take the hose from the pumper through a convenient gap between the wheels and pump oil into each axlebox until full up to the level of the cork.

The bogie is next on the list; there are no water drain plugs on these axleboxes, so the two corks are simply removed and oil pumped into one using the fingers to seal the nozzle until it starts to run out of the other. Then a splash in each of the four corks on top of the spring hangers to complete the job.

And now for the really dirty bit! The Mid-Hants does not have enough volunteers to afford the luxury of full time cleaners and so the only filth that ever gets removed from the inside motion is what gets wiped off on the driver's overalls each time he oils round! There are two corks each on the eccentric and the expansion link and one each on the big end, radius rod and small end to contend with, plus the die blocks and an oil hole for the slide bars. There is supposed to an optimum position of the wheels so that all these points are within easy reach - if so, I have yet to find where it is! Firstly you will have to mountaineer up into the works, scrabbling with your feet on the brake rigging, springs and frame stretchers, whilst hauling yourself up by the arms on the oily motion work. If you are lucky, you may find you can reach both eccentric corks and the big end from the back, but in my case the front eccentric cork is usually just out of reach and I have to climb down again and then repeat the process from the other side, which will mean wriggling right in over the connecting rod. Having done these three, it will be necessary to reposition yourself again for the remainder. With the job nearly completed, Sod's Law now dictates that this is the moment when you will drop a cork down into the pit amongst the ash and filth and will have to climb down to retrieve it and back up yet again - this is guaranteed to use up any swear words you may still have left in your vocabulary!

The final job is back on the footplate, where a small plug has to be removed from a pipe so that some cylinder oil can be poured in to lubricate the steam brake. Bob Deeth had been watching my efforts and now asked whether I had finished. When I said yes, he then took great delight in pointing out two small holes on the tender brake shaft which I had missed! Having attended to these, the job really was completed and I retired to the 'Manor' for a wash up and a change of overalls.

Back on the engine again with Bob observing my every move, I checked the brakes before giving the whistle a toot and backing up along the pit road to give the boiler a blowdown. This done, we waited for the dummy to clear and ran down to the signal box where we collected the token, before trundling off down to Alresford to rendezvous with our train. This happened to be berthed in the down platform, so the first job was to drag it out up the line past the crossover and then put it back in platform 1, which is where we normally started from. While doing this, I was looking back down the train to spot the red flag from the guard, to tell us we were clear of the points, rather than watching where we were in relation to the advanced starting signal which was at danger; I knew that we would not run past it with a train of this length, but the fact I wasn't watching out earned me the first black mark of the day.

Leaving Alresford, the gradient eases as you come out of the cutting and the train will accelerate quite rapidly. Under normal circumstances you would normally just let the engine go at this point, knowing that the speed would soon be brought back when the steeper bit is reached. As this was my test, however, there was no way I was going to exceed the speed limit, so I shut the regulator well down to make sure we remained strictly legal; unfortunately I was a bit slow opening up again and we actually lost a few mph - another black mark. The day had turned out to be rather wet and I was a bit concerned that we might have trouble slipping. What with that and the fact that the regulator on *Bodmin* was very stiff and required both hands to open and shut it, I decided to run with about three-quarter regulator and 35 to 40 per cent cut-off on the climb out of Ropley, so that if we slipped (and we did), then I would be able to shut off that much quicker - Bob didn't think much of that idea either, although he saved all these criticisms until after we have finished and gone back to the 'Manor'.

Actually the argument as to whether it is best to run with a fully open regulator and short cut-off, or a smaller regulator opening and longer cut-off has divided enginemen for generations. It can be proved in theory and has been demonstrated in tests, that the former method will be more economical on coal and water, but this is not the only consideration. Certainly, if the engine is one of the more modern types with long travel valves and is in good condition, then the full regulator argument is pretty convincing. Older and more run down engines will often start knocking in the axleboxes if they are pulled up too tight and will be a lot more comfortable running with a longer cut-off, which gives a more even pressure in the cylinders. After watching Bob (Cartwright) do it for years I am normally a full regulator man, but on this particular occasion, opted to do it the other way.

The only other incident of note during the test occurred down at Alton, where we had unhooked and were ready to run round the train. *Bodmin*, with exquisite timing, decided that this was the moment she would refuse to start. I gave the regulator a pull and nothing happened, so I gave it a bigger one - still nothing. Normally at this stage, the only thing to do is to set back a few feet the wrong way, before whipping the reverser over again and having another go. We couldn't do this however, because we were still buffered up against a train with its brakes hard on! Bob watched me struggle for a bit and then said, 'Let me have it'. Basically he did the same things as me but with more violence - I think that finally he managed to drive *Bodmin* forward into the train hard enough to compress the buffer springs, so that when he wound the reverser back again they pushed us off, anyway, we had got moving again.

The author firing *Bodmin* in 2005 – I seem to have got her rather hot!   *P. Goodworth*

Engine driver at last! The author, with *Bodmin* in 2005.   *P. Goodworth*

After this little contretemps, the rest of the trip passed uneventfully. I had managed to stop in all the right places, including the water stop, which was spot on and when we got back to Ropley and let the regular driver have his engine back, I was feeling fairly satisfied with my efforts. We went back to Bob's office in the 'Manor' for a debrief and for the next 15 minutes Bob spelled out to me all the aforementioned faults, plus a few more besides, in very fine detail. Apart from telling me that my speed keeping downhill had been very good, it was all negative and for a while I thought it meant I had failed. Right at the very end, however, Bob finally got round to telling me he was going to pass me out. I have to say that as I drove home I was feeling more depressed than elated, despite all the handshakes and pats on the back I got from the other chaps in the shed before I left. For a day or two after this I brooded about some of the things he had said and actually started to wonder whether I still wanted to be on the Railway. But the bottom line was that I had been passed out. Being an engine driver is a position of great responsibility - and Bob's neck would also be on the line if I screwed up, so he had to be tough. After some thought, I decided that having got this far it would be silly to pack it in just because of some criticism, most of which I deserved anyway, so I would carry on for a few more turns and see how things went.

A couple of weeks passed and then it was time for my first driving turn - another wet day and *Bodmin* once again. I was feeling pretty nervous at first and double-checked everything before moving off shed, but as soon as we got away from Alresford with the first train of the day I started to relax and simply got on with job. It was a very lonely feeling, to be sitting in the driver's seat without Bob Cartwright's friendly figure beside me to give the odd word of advice, or simply a joke about 'negative boiler control' if I was few pounds short of steam. My fireman, who I had never met before, was Roger Latch, who was once himself a footplateman based at Reading and had plenty of experience, so I had no worries about his side of the job. Regrettably, Roger had decided to give up the railway as he was finding the long trip to and from his home in Bath a bit of a struggle, so this turned out to be the one and only time we went out together.

Remembering the other Bob's criticism, I worked the engine all day with the regulator handle pushed right up to the roof and between 25 and 35 per cent cut-off on the banks - *Bodmin* didn't slip once! At the end of the day, which had been completely uneventful, I felt quite a bit happier about the whole business and found my enthusiasm returning. I thanked Roger for his efforts on my maiden trip and wished him well for the future. I could tell by the look on his face that he was already having some regrets about leaving but, as if to burn his boats, he now presented me with his nearly new Beesley shovel as a generous parting gift.

One thing that I did find hard was that my regular fireman Rob Forster was quite often unavailable because he was actually rostered out on two crews and couldn't always get the necessary time off work. When he was there he was very good but when he wasn't I was often teamed up with a virtual stranger. Altogether during my first year as a driver I went out with nine different firemen, most of whom were fine but it was rather difficult to strike up much of a rapport with any of them when you only went out once or twice together.

Stanier 'Black Five' No. 45231 *Sherwood Forester* runs round the train past the water tower at Alton in 2005.   *Keith Stockley*

Stanier 'Black Five' 4-6-0 No. 45231 *Sherwood Forester* leaving Ropley in 2005.   *Tony Wood*

On the locomotive front the opposite was true and I seemed to spend nearly the entire year on *Bodmin* - oh boy, did I get to detest that inside valve gear! By way of a slight variation, I did get two turns on *Canadian Pacific*, which of course has pretty much the same oiling routine to go through. If you put a 'Merchant Navy' and one of the smaller 'West Country' Pacifics side by side, they look nearly identical but you will find that the 'Merchant Navy' has one extra wash-out plug on the side of the firebox just above the handrail, which is one of the give aways. Apart from the longer firebox, the boiler barrel of the 'Merchant Navy' has a slightly bigger diameter as well. This means that the inside expansion link is now so close to the bottom of the boiler, that when you have mountaineered up there with the oil feeder to attend to the two corks as previously described, you will find that you will be unable to tip the feeder up enough to get any oil to run out and will have to climb down again to fetch a squirt can or the hose from the pumper instead - I tell you, these engines are great fun to drive but can be seriously bad for the blood pressure!

One locomotive I had been looking forward to having a go on was LMS 'Black Five' 4-6-0 No. 45231, which had been named *Sherwood Forester* after coming into private ownership. The nickname 'Black Five' which was universally used, came about simply because they were power classification 5 (Freight) and were painted black. They were certainly the most well-known of any mixed traffic design to run in Britain and were so successful that the London, Midland & Scottish Railway eventually built 842 of them!

It is not difficult to see why they were so popular on the LMS if one looks back a little to see what there was before. The LMS had been formed at the Grouping of 1923 by the amalgamation of several large railway companies including the Midland and the London & North Western, none of which had much in the way of modern superheated engines. The LNWR had a few 'Claughton' four-cylinder 4-6-0s dating back to 1912, but otherwise nearly everything was being hauled around by elderly 4-4-0s and 0-6-0s, whose lineage dated back to Victorian times. The Midland in particular had always been a small engine railway and nearly all its express trains were double-headed - it is amazing to think they could still make a profit with such uneconomical methods. After the Grouping when Henry Fowler took over as chief mechanical engineer, nothing much changed to start with and his first contribution was to build yet another 580 0-6-0 goods engines; these class '4Fs' were really just superheated versions of some earlier Derby (Midland) designs. Although they were capable of hauling heavy goods trains, their small wheels and limited boiler capacity meant they were no use on any passenger service and the cabs seemed to be designed in order to maximise discomfort for the crew - if these were the only engines left in preservation I don't think I would have bothered becoming a railwayman. Fowler went on to produce some better engines and is particularly remembered for the 'Royal Scot' 4-6-0s but it was his successor, William Stanier (later Sir William Stanier FRS) who really gave the LMS the engines it needed.

Stanier's career originated on the Great Western, which at the time of the Grouping was at the forefront of locomotive design. GWR locomotives, though, were stuck in a time warp dating back to Churchward's era. The 'Castles' of

1923 were really just enlarged 'Stars' of 1906 and the 'Kings' which appeared in 1927 were simply bigger again, while the mixed traffic 'Hall' class 4-6-0s were actually just Churchward 'Saints' with smaller wheels. They all had inside valve gear and low levels of superheat which were state of the art in 1906 but had become a little dated 20 years later. When Stanier moved over to take over the LMS in 1932 he took the best of Great Western practice with him and added a few improvements of his own. Whilst retaining the classic Swindon boiler with its taper barrel and Belpaire (flat-topped) firebox, he finally put the valve gear outside where it belonged and installed a more comfortable and user friendly cab. A 'Black Five' then is really just a GWR 'Hall' with outside valve gear, slightly more superheat and an improved cab and tender; paint one green and the similarity would be obvious! They immediately proved to be most capable and versatile engines and could be found hauling anything from humble freights to express passenger trains with equal success.

For my driving turn on No. 45231, I was paired up with Duncan Richardson (no relation) as fireman, who turned out to be a most willing and helpful mate. The 'Black Five' did everything asked of it without fuss and we enjoyed a very easy and uneventful day.

I know that at this point I am going to upset quite a number of die-hard LMS fans but now I have had personal experience of both this engine and the very similar BR Standard class '5', I am bound to say that the 'Standard 5' is the better engine. Just as Stanier had updated the GWR 'Hall' in 1934, by 1950 things had moved on again, and Mr Riddles and his team were able to make a number of small but collectively significant improvements to the 'Black Five'. The cylinders were nearly identical but the valve travel on the 'Standard 5' was considerably longer, which meant that the engine could be notched up further without adversely affecting the speed at which steam could get in and out of the cylinders. The axles now ran in roller bearings which meant less friction; it is very noticeable when buffering up to a train how long the Standard engine will keep rolling on just a puff of steam. The driving wheels are also two inches bigger in diameter on the later engine but this really will not mean much in terms of speed. In the cab, it all boils down to personal preferences and I think that the pull up regulator and 'bacon slicer' reverser wheel are easier to get on with than the push across lever and transverse wheel on the 'Black Five'. The only difference that really matters however, is how the engines compare on the road and I found that the 'Black Five' needed to be thumped a lot harder than the Standard to do the same job - typically 10 per cent more cut-off in fact, which I think proves the point.

During my first few months as a driver, all my turns had been fairly straightforward but these are not the ones that make interesting reading. Eventually I had a rough one, in the shape of a Real Ale Train (RAT). These trains are very well patronised and usually consist of seven coaches instead of the normal five, so they can be quite a challenge, especially if it is a wet day. Our engine was *Bodmin* yet again, but as we didn't take over until the afternoon, it meant that on this occasion I escaped the chore of oiling round underneath. We did have to clean the fire before we started, however. The off-going crew had warned us that the coal tended to produce a lot of ash and a squint in the firebox confirmed this. To clean the fire, we opened the ashpan and rocked the firebars on the left hand side of the firebox, thereby dumping all the remaining fire and ash into the pit. After this, the various fire irons were used to scrape away the remaining ash from around the sides of the box and to knock any odd bits of clinker off the bars. Then we closed the grate again and used the clinker shovel (always called the paddle for some strange reason) to ladle the remaining fire across onto the clean side. The right-hand side could then be treated in the same way. Finally, the remaining fire was spread around and we could start building it up again. By the time we had done this, there was actually very little fire left, so we had to go and collect some wood to speed the relighting process.

By the time we had completed this hot and sweaty performance, we just had time for a quick wash before collecting the train and taking it to Alton, where the service starts and finishes. My fireman, whom I shall not name, was yet another unfamiliar face to me but he seemed to be keen enough, so I left him to get on with building up the fire for departure while I hooked on and got the tea. When I came back, my new mate was just adding the last few shovelfuls; I thought it could have done with a bit more in view of the heavy load but said nothing - different fireman use different methods and perhaps he preferred to leave it until we got going. When we got the 'right away' and started to accelerate up the 1 in 100, all seemed to be well at first and the pressure started to rise; I was about to remind the fireman to put the injector on to avoid blowing off but was just too late and the safeties lifted. By the time the valves had sat down again we had lost 15 lb. of steam, which as it turned out we could certainly have done with later on. The fireman however, obviously thought that things were well under control and proceeded to pour himself a cup of tea! I soon disabused him of this idea and told him to get stoking, which he did, but even with the injector shut off, the pressure did not rise again and by the time we were over Butts and onto the steep part of the bank it was definitely on its way down.

My fireman was now working hard but appeared to be fighting a losing battle. I suggested that it was probably the back corners that were the problem but it is difficult to get any there when the engine is working hard and I suspected that most of his shots were being dragged forward by the blast and were fetching up somewhere down the sides. I worked the engine as easily as possible but the pressure declined all the way; by the time we reached the racetrack, which is the normal point at which you stop firing, I was beginning to wonder if we were going to make it without having to stop for a blow-up, as the pressure was already down to 160, with the water coming back into sight in the glass. The speed had fallen to 20 mph at this point but even with full regulator and 45 per cent cut-off we were still decelerating slowly so I couldn't ease off any more. By the time we staggered past Medstead distant at around 10 mph, things were looking very grim; the pressure was now below 150 and I was watching the vacuum gauge like a hawk in case I needed the large ejector to keep the brakes off. Finally, the welcome sight of 'Thank Christ' bridge appeared round the bend and after a few more laboured beats from the chimney I could shut off; this immediately caused the water level to drop to about an inch in the glass which was not enough to go over the top, so I had to crawl all the way over the summit and down into Medstead at below walking pace, to allow the injectors time to raise it to a safe level again.

Remembering the forbearance Bob had shown to me when I had been in similar situations, I refrained from saying much to my somewhat crestfallen mate, beyond the obvious comment that it had been much too close for comfort. While we freewheeled down to Ropley, the fireman set about repairing the fire, which as I had suspected had virtually disappeared from the back corners of the box.

Down at Alresford, we managed a fairly quick turn round, while my mate had another go at building the fire. The only advice I gave was to repeat what Dave Sibley had said to me 10 years earlier, which was to 'Keep stuffing the back corners until you think they're full, then stuff them some more'. While he was doing this, one of our passengers, who by now was already somewhat the worse for drink, came up to the cab to remind us to make sure we had the spring wound up properly this time!

The return trip was definitely an improvement but still not great; this time when we arrived back at Medstead we had 180 lb. of steam and half a glass of water, having lost still more time. I had already decided, however, that it was time to do a bit of 'leading from the front' and told the fireman that I would make up the fire for the next trip up from Alton; apart from anything else it was turning out to be a really cold night and I felt like a bit of exercise. As soon as we had run round the train I set to with the shovel and whacked about 30 shots into each back corner just for starters. Then I piled on a great big heap just under the door and a dozen down each side to complete the classic 'horseshoe' shaped fire. Giving the shovel back to my mate with the instruction to wait until I gave him the tip and then to fire about six at a time across the width of the box, letting the blast take it down the slope, I went back to my seat feeling a whole lot warmer.

By now it was completely dark, which was also a first for me as driver but I was feeling fairly confident that we were going to have a better trip this time. At the 'right away' I gave the whistle a blast and put 'Bodmin' to work. As soon as the tail of the train cleared the points, I heaved the regulator wide open and wound the reverser back to 45 per cent, which soon had us accelerating nicely. The pressure started to rise as well but this time my mate was ready for it and quickly put on an injector; I was pleased to see that the pressure continued to hold at 240 against the injector, so we were off to a good start. I gave my mate the nod to get stoking and then stuck my head outside to try and make out any landmarks.

Although it wasn't actually raining, it had been very cloudy, so it was a pitch black night and after we left the lights of Alton behind, it was so dark I couldn't see even the faintest hint of the shining rails out in front of us. Apart from the cinders that had found their way past the wire mesh grids in the smokebox and had been shot out the chimney leaving rocket trails, the only other light came from the partly open firedoors, which sent brilliant orange beams out from the cab and into the surrounding blackness - all very romantic but not actually much good to see by. Every time I turned back into cab to look at the gauges I would lose my night vision again and would be nearly blind when I returned my attention to the road. Not for the first time, I marvelled at the ability of the steam drivers in the old days, who sometimes had hundreds of miles of route knowledge and could run trains at express speeds day or night, knowing exactly where to look to pick out the dim glimmer of oil lit signal lamps.

Our trip this time was turning out to be just fine - *Bodmin* was hustling our seven coaches up the hill in grand style, my mate was keeping the pressure up against the injector and had obviously started to enjoy himself again, while I could begin to relax as well. When we had run round the train at Alresford for the last trip back, Ian Cooper who is another of our footplate inspectors, came up to me and reminded me 'not to hang about' on the return, to ensure we arrived in time to connect with the last main line service out of Alton. This was just the sort of encouragement we needed and my fireman busied himself in piling on a whacking great fire which had me nodding my head in approval for a change. Our return journey was also quite uneventful and we rolled down into Alton with four minutes to spare before the South West Trains service was due to depart. The only thing left now was to wait while our well-oiled punters disembarked and then we could take the empty stock back to Ropley and ensure 'Bodmin' was screwed down securely on the pit road.

By the time I had finished writing up the engine report card and had a wash to remove at least the first layer of grime, it was 1 am and I was feeling rather weary, so I made myself a cup of coffee before starting the long drive home. In the car I was reflecting on what had been a pretty demanding turn and for the first time I began to feel that I really had become an engine driver at last.

What now? Well, there are still plenty of engines I would love to have a go on. Being a fan of the BR Standards, a 'Britannia' is probably top of the wish list, together with a Stanier Pacific - it would be interesting to compare the latter with an 'A4' as both types have a great number of fans, who will never agree as to which is the finest passenger engine in the country. Personally, I think that *Tornado*, which is the Peppercorn 'A1' Pacific being built from scratch, will turn out to be better than either of them, but that opinion is bound to set off yet another round of controversy. Another firm favourite is the Southern 'Schools' class 4-4-0 and purely for nostalgic reasons, the GWR *City of Truro*, which has visited the Mid-Hants once but I didn't get a chance to go out on it. There may still be time: provided I can keep passing the annual medical I should have at least six more years driving, by which time the steam bug may finally be out of my system – although I doubt it!

Ex-LSWR 0-4-0T No. 96 *Normandy* beside the water tower at Ropley.   *Author*

Visiting GWR 0-6-0 Saddle tank No. 813 in 2004. Bob and the author got her so hot on one run up to Medstead, that the baffle plate melted and disappeared without trace!   *Gwen Cartwright*

Appendix

List of Locomotives fired or driven by the Author

Locomotive	Comments
'Thomas'	'J94' class 0-6-0 saddle tank converted to side tanks.
'Douglas'	'J94' class 0-6-0 converted to a tender engine.
'Percy'	Peckett 0-4-0 saddle tank No. 1728.
96	LSWR 0-4-0 tank *Normandy*.
813	GWR 0-6-0 saddle tank.
3278	Baldwin 'S160' class 2-8-0 *Franklin D. Roosevelt*.
5029	GWR 'Castle' class 4-6-0 *Nunney Castle*.
5080	GWR 'Castle' class 4-6-0 *Defiant*.
5764	GWR 0-6-0 pannier tank.
6024	GWR 'King' class 4-6-0 *King Edward I*.
30506	SR 'S15' class 4-6-0.
31625	SR 'U' class 2-6-0.
31874	SR 'N' class 2-6-0.
32473	LBSCR 'E4' class 0-6-2T.
34007	SR 'West Country' class 4-6-2 *Wadebridge*.
34016	SR Rebuilt 'West Country' class 4-6-2 *Bodmin*.
34105	SR 'West Country' class 4-6-2 *Swanage*.
35005	SR 'Merchant Navy' class 4-6-2 *Canadian Pacific*.
41312	LMS Ivatt class '2' 2-6-2 tank engine.
45231	LMS Stanier 'Black Five' 4-6-0 *Sherwood Forester*.
60007	LNER Gresley 'A4' 4-6-2 *Sir Nigel Gresley*.
60009	LNER Gresley 'A4' 4-6-2 *Union of South Africa*.
60019	LNER Gresley 'A4' 4-6-2 *Bittern*.
73096	BR Standard class '5' 4-6-0.
80151	BR Standard class '4' 2-6-4 tank engine.
92203	BR Standard class '9F' 2-10-0 *Black Prince*.
92212	BR Standard class '9F' 2-10-0.

As the book was completed by December 2005 but not published until 2008, there are several engines in the above list that are not mentioned in the text.

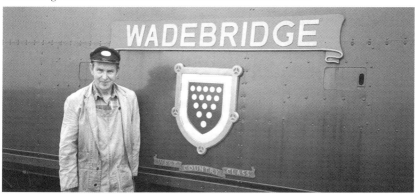

The author with *Wadebridge*.   *Author's Collection*

Bob Cartwright and the author with No. 73096.

Author's Collection